This book is dedicated to all of my family,
Nancy my wife, Nevin, Jason and Paula, Bryan, and Braeden
my first grandson, my parents John and Rita, who always
tried to encourage me throughout life and Mark.

THE TICKING TIME BOMB

By
Michael J. Woulas, Ph.D.

This book is not meant to be a substitute for medical care of people with bipolar disorder or depression and treatment should not be based solely on its contents.

© 2010 by Michael J. Woulas, PhD.
All Rights Reserved. No part of this book may be reproduced, stored in a retrieval system, or transmitted by any means. (i.e. electronic, mechanical, photocopying, recording, or otherwise, without written permission from the author.

Cover Design by Kara Campbell, Whirlwind Media Services

Edited by Mary Nelson-Haffner

Published by Lulu Publishing & Lattitude Media, August 2010, **ISBN 978-0-557-54747-0**

Copies of this book are available at: www.hereishelp.net
Downloadable copies are also available.
Email your comments and feedback to:
info@hereishelp.net

ACKNOWLEDGMENTS

I would like to thank all the patients and their families who have shared their sorrows and their joys trying to deal with Bipolar Disorder, Type II. Most of my learning has come from the clinical experiences they have given me since 2004.

I would also like to thank Mary Haffner for her expertise and assistance as a marketing and media professional for the ongoing review and editing process, including her prior publishing experience.

Thanks to Karen Campbell of Cam-Bel Media for her unique design of the book cover. Also thanks to Jack Campbell for inspiring Karen and the team at Cam-Bel Media.

Finally, thanks to the editing readers who dedicated time and energy to provide editing input and general comments on the manuscript and the book project itself.

There were many others who offered important suggestions, comments, and great encouragement as I shared my ideas and purposes for this book. They also deserve thanks and appreciation for what they provided during this process.

TABLE OF CONTENTS

CHAPTER 1 — 1
FAMILY EXPOSURE TO ANGER AND RAGE STEMMING FROM BIPOLAR DISORDER, TYPE II
- Importance of family stability
- Anger is a basic human emotion
- The family member with anger and rage
- Effects of anger and rage on the family

CHAPTER 2 — 21
UNDERSTANDING MOOD DISORDERS
- Defining normal moods
- Types of mood disorders

CHAPTER 3 — 39
BIPOLAR DISORDER, TYPE II & THE MISDIAGNOSED PROBLEM OF THE CENTURY
- Misconceptions of bipolar depression
- Bipolar depression vs. manic depression
- Basic symptoms of bipolar depression
- Stress is a trigger for mood disorders
- Defining stress

CHAPTER 4 — 59
ABUSE IN THE FAMILY ASSOCIATED WITH BIPOLAR DISORDER, TYPE II
- Disrupted family systems
- Common sources of family stress
- The family abuser
- Types of family abuse
- Substance abuse and bipolar depression
- Abuse and the family scapegoat

CHAPTER 5   73
BIPOLAR DISORDER, TYPE II AND THE DEVELOPMENT OF CODEPENDENCY

    Codependency history

    Personality traits of codependency

    Negative thinking

    Fears and anxiety

CHAPTER 6   89
PROCESS OF HEALING FROM BIPOLAR DISORDER, TYPE II

    Dynamics of hurt and emotional pain

    Cognitive-behavioral therapy

    Insight psychotherapy

    Treating the whole family

    Alternative assistance

    Medication for depression and anxiety

CHAPTER 7   109
SOCIAL AND LEGAL CONSEQUENCES OF BIPOLAR DEPRESSION, TYPE II

    The criminal justice system

    The anger management approach

    Drug and alcohol counseling approaches

    Mass murder epidemic

ABC'S OF EMOTION   119
WOULAS BIPOLAR DISORDER. TYPE II EVALUATION SCALE [WBPIIS]   121
ABOUT THE AUTHOR   124

An Introduction By The Author

In the winter of 2004, an article from a medical journal on bipolar depression or Bipolar Disorder, Type II came across my desk. Like most other clinicians, I was trained to identify Bipolar Disorder, Type I or manic-depression. However, the Type II classification was basically omitted from my training. I had never encountered such a clear and concise description of this common mood disorder, which has escaped awareness by most medical and psychological practitioners.

I had over 24 years of experience at that time treating mood disorders and anxiety, but never understood that bipolar depression was an actual clinical entity. As I read this journal article, it became clear I was in the dark when it came to diagnosing and treating this condition. I obtained only brief and superficial exposure to Bipolar Disorder, Type II, while studying the Diagnostic and Statistical Manual and never really associated it with the depression I was seeing in the office. However, I was very aware of the fact that many depressed patients did not seem to get well, despite receiving good psychotherapy and the best medications available for depression and anxiety.

The article went on to explain that patients with bipolar depression are generally misdiagnosed with unipolar depression and anxiety. Their condition may worsen over time and many end up taking their own lives and the lives of others through murder and suicide. The fact is that any bipolar mood disorder will not improve without utilizing a class of medications referred to as mood stabilizers. Most of those with Bipolar, Type II illness have never been treated with a mood stabilizer and the focus has been on reducing anxiety with Benzodiazepines such as Xanax and treatment of the depression with SSRI's such as Prozac, Effexor or Zoloft. These medicines offer minimal help and the agitation, irritability, anger and rage associated with Bipolar Disorder, Type II will progressively worsen over time.

    I began paying closer attention to my patients who had a chronic depressive history, despite being treated for years by many clinicians with these medications and psychotherapies. They all seemed to have similar and unresolved symptoms including; mood swings, irritability, agitation, racing thoughts, depression and rage episodes. I came to the conclusion that these patients were misdiagnosed with depression and anxiety and they were, in fact, the type of patients discussed in the journal article. The absence of full-blown manic episodes was a major reason for the misdiagnoses. Further research, which was sparse and difficult to find confirmed what was reported.

    Misdiagnosis of bipolar depression has been partly responsible for the epidemic of domestic violence, substance abuse and more importantly, destruction of the family unit. Families of an individual with bipolar depression are highly susceptible to frequent episodes of verbal and physical abuse. The psychological damage to these family members can be severe because of the high levels of fear, depression and co-dependency it causes.

The judicial system has been dealing with the cycle of domestic violence and substance abuse associated with bipolar depression for many decades through referral to anger management and mental health recovery programs. Ironically, most of these programs fail to correctly identify the root problem, which is bipolar depression.

"The Ticking Time Bomb," is a title created specifically to exemplify the emotional condition of each individual with Bipolar Disorder, Type II. The explosive anger, rage and abuse are characteristic of a "time bomb" ready to detonate with dangerous and serious consequences, not only for the individual, but also, for those within the immediate environment.

The explosiveness of most individuals with bipolar depression can be diffused and can improve, provided it is correctly diagnosed. Bipolar Disorder, Type II is hereditary and a medical condition which can be triggered by minimal levels of stress. Changes in brain chemistry occur following exposure to stress, which causes racing thoughts, mood swings, anger, rage and depression. This is not an ordinary type of depression, anxiety or a personality disorder, which it is so often confused with by healthcare professionals. This is a bipolar mood disorder, which needs to be correctly identified and treated. People with this disorder can improve and live a more healthy and productive life with proper diagnosis and treatment.

HereisHelp.net has been established, in part to help generate greater public awareness of bipolar depression. We have been successfully treating this condition since 2004 and hope to reach greater numbers through our web based information and services. Many more articles, webinars, podcasts, DVD's and this book on Bipolar Disorder, Type II are becoming available to help reduce the epidemic of rage and violence facing our world.

Michael J. Woulas, Ph.D.

CHAPTER 1
Family Exposure to Anger and Rage Stemming from Bipolar Disorder, Type II

"Barbara seemed to have, just beneath the surface, this anger that would very easily burst out. It would be displayed most of the time in nastiness, and 'put-downs'. This was mainly directed at me, although on occasion others would be in the line of fire. Sometimes, her words would be more directed at me, like 'I wish you were dead,' or 'wish you would just go to hell.' Like with Karen, it become so that even in our good times, I would wonder when the next upset would come," Leon.

Importance of Family Stability

Families are the basic building blocks of society and maintaining family stability is essential for our long-term survival. The emotional health of the family is contingent upon certain conditions such as respect and personal validity. Effective communication including the ability to solve problems contributes greatly to family stability. Communication and problem solving skills of the family requires successful completion of three basic steps. These steps involve listening, processing and a proper response to others.

Listening is basic to effective communication and begins with turning off one's own ideas and opinions, while focusing on what the other person is trying to say. Many of us while listening to others quickly formulate our own opinions and we look for a quick opportunity to interject them. This is not considered effective listening. Important thoughts and feelings of a family member are reflected in their words. In order to communicate with others we need to focus on and pay attention to what is being expressed through their words.

Processing accurately and understanding what is being said follows the listening phase. Processing verbal expression occurs as you put personal opinions aside. It also requires a level of respect, concern and attention to what is important to a family member. This occurs best when one's personal views are set aside. Processing requires a high level of respect, interest and focus on what others in the family believe to be important.

An appropriate response to what is heard and understood is the final step in healthy communication and problem solving. A positive response requires listening and in-depth comprehension. A productive response in the communication process occurs when the one listening maintains rational and realistic perceptions of the situation. Also, healthy responses occur more often when the individuals in the family strive to be positive and calm. Some degree of emotionally charged responses during communication and problem solving is normal for every family. However, stability of the family is dependent upon respect and validation of its members. Unhealthy emotions, such as prolonged fear, anger and rage will most assuredly disrupt any phase of communication and decrease the stability of the family.

Anger is a Basic Human Emotion

Human beings are emotional creatures capable of expressing thoughts and feelings. Emotions can vary from healthy, such as peacefulness, joy and love, to unhealthy, such as fear, sadness and anger. Variations of emotion are common. They tend to reflect changes in the conditions of the environment. Most human emotions are governed by thoughts or perceptions of each situation encountered at any moment in time.

Human emotion is also personal and unique to each individual. For example, two people can experience a situation simultaneously and have very different emotional experiences. This phenomenon has been of interest to behavioral scientists for quite some time. More recently, researchers began to scientifically investigate these differences with studies involving both human and animal emotion. The conclusions drawn from decades of study confirm that variations of thought and perception actually generate the emotional responses of subjects exposed to identical situations.

Healthy human emotion has a very positive impact on the family. The expression of love through kindness, affection, understanding and acceptance builds confidence, independence and personal success. Joy, happiness and peace-of-mind, are all healthy emotional states. They contribute to the establishment and maintenance of functional patterns in the family. Sadness, fear and anger, which sound negative, may also serve individuals and families in a positive way. Fear may alert families to some potentially dangerous events. Anger may also produce a defensive or an offensive response when a family is protecting itself from a threat.

In many cases, an emotion such as anger can develop into an unhealthy condition. Fear, sadness and anger are all considered basic human emotions. However, they easily become unhealthy, if they are unresolved over a period of time. Escalation, intensification and the increase in frequency of anger may give rise to serious behavioral health problems. Most families are exposed at one time or another to someone with similar anger and rage-related problems.

Family Member with Anger and Rage

Hardly a family escapes the experience of living with someone who has difficulty managing their anger. Many families have one or more members who have periodic episodes of anger and rage. Typically, young children at two or three years of age go through a developmental stage where they often exhibit temper tantrums. These episodes are usually preceded by a person of authority placing some form of limitation on their behavior. For example, "You cannot have ice cream before your dinner". This type of positive restriction or limit setting creates frustration in the child, which often leads to an outburst of angry emotion. With patience, and at times the use of logical consequences for destructive anger, the child grows out of this stage.

Anger, rage and bipolar depression often begin to manifest during this stage of development. Children at this early age, who do not respond to limits and logical consequences following severe tantrums, continue with these behaviors. Daycare and pre-school staff may report that the child bites, fights and is generally very difficult to manage if they do not get their way.

This particular child may be predisposed to a mood related problem. Look at older siblings, parents and grandparents for some apparent history of mood disorder, which may be linked to the child's problems. It is not uncommon in some families to have both biological parents with an anger, rage and depression history. These family members with rage and anger find it difficult to avoid arguments and have trouble solving ordinary family problems.

Effects of Anger and Rage on the Family

The rage and anger of bipolar depression are usually projected onto family members. These unhealthy emotions take many forms such as verbal threats and destruction of household objects. Assigning blame to others for family problems is also very common. Finger pointing with accusations such as "you're the problem, not me" or "You're the reason I'm like I am" become frequently heard expressions. Those who live with blame and finger pointing over time begin to believe that the accusations are true. They become convinced they are responsible for existing problems in the relationship and for the actions of others. They try endlessly to improve themselves hoping to please the angry person and to prevent further rages from occurring.

Normal conflicts and family differences may

quickly turn into angry confrontations. Battles often ensue over who is right or wrong in the conflict. Anger can rapidly escalate into rage. The bipolar person generally has poor regulatory skills in these situations. At this point of heightened emotional volatility families are at the greatest risk for violence and abuse. Depending on the severity of the bipolar condition, any or all individuals in view become targets. These conditions are becoming extraordinarily common today and often require domestic violence intervention by law enforcement and the courts.

A major mistake in our criminal justice system occurs when the bipolar person is assigned to an anger management program, which generally fails to recognize the biological and medical aspects of the problem. It is astonishing how widespread failure to identify domestic violence as a bipolar mood problem is leading to frequent assaults and loss of life. Innocent and unprotected families are exposed to repeat episodes of abuse, violence and death because the offender is considered to have an anger problem and not severe bipolar depression.

Families are Mini-Organizations

Most families today are made up of three or more members each with designated roles and duties. Viewing the family as an organization similar to a small business allows us to appreciate the importance of a family system. Families have been studied in the context of a system for several decades. The term "system" is used to describe sets of rules, policies, goals and objectives, which are uniquely created by each family. The more functional and effective the family system becomes, the more successful they are at achieving their established goals.

Understanding the family system requires close scrutiny of the communication patterns between all members of the family. Patterns of communication evolve over time and are referred to as either functional or dysfunctional. Unhealthy family systems develop as a consequence of dysfunctional communication patterns. Families with more functional patterns communicate more effectively, particularly when difficult and stressful conditions exist. Functional patterns generally reflect a higher level of rational and logical thinking. The healthy emotions, which follow are more appropriate and contribute greatly to a functional system.

Dysfunctional patterns of communication often evolve when one family member acquires an unhealthy emotional condition such as bipolar depression. In other words, excessive anger, rage, and mood swings in one family member create dysfunctional patterns of communication throughout the whole family system. As a result, the emotional health and wellbeing of all family members are adversely affected. Healthy individuals within the family acquire negative thought processes, which generate unhealthy emotions such as fear, anger and sadness. These members of the family eventually develop poor coping skills and mismanage important situations, including difficult and challenging experiences.

Stress Caused by Bipolar Depression

Stress occurs from many sources if a family member has undiagnosed Bipolar Disorder, Type II. A parent may have difficulty maintaining steady employment, which often places the family under significant financial stress. Loss of employment generally occurs due to anger and noncompliance in the workplace. Relationships with an employer or other employees may begin on good terms, but rapidly deteriorates due to the individual's overly critical and often inappropriate attitude. Arguments, frequent complaints, fighting and missed workdays are common reasons for loss of employment.

Emotional volatility is another major source of stress on the family. The bipolar depressed person is like living with a time bomb ready to explode. They are very emotionally unpredictable. The slightest occurrences can produce rage. Simply being in the presence of a person with this type of history is a stressful event for most family members. Children with bipolar depression have serious difficulties academically, which become stressful on parents and the whole family. Poor academic achievement, fighting, truancy, class disruption and excessive administrative discipline are common stressors. These children are frequently misdiagnosed with ADD or ADHD and fail to respond to customary forms of treatment, which often create high stress levels for the parents.

Prolonged stress from bipolar depression in most cases will create conflict and disruption in the family. Marital conflicts between husband and wife tend to escalate, especially if one or both have an undiagnosed mood disorder. A typical couple under these stressful conditions will experience frequent arguments, abuse of alcohol or drugs, verbal and physical abuse, all of which leads to some form of domestic violence. Children become exposed through direct observation and in many instances become active participants. It is not uncommon for a child to begin defending a parent who is being subjected to verbal and physical abuse. A child may step in-between parents or the couple during these episodes and make verbal threats toward the abuser. Placing oneself in this position will appear as though the child is siding with one against the other. This usually intensifies the anger and rage of the affected adults, which places the child in a dangerous position.

These highly dysfunctional patterns in the family become routine over time. Unfortunately, many children exposed to the anger and rages of bipolar depression begin to accept this as normal family functioning. It is not until early adolescence and having experienced more healthy families that these children begin to see what has been seriously wrong with their own family. Those who do not make this connection may continue to believe that their family experiences are normal everyday events and just part of life.

In these cases, we see that the high level of stress on families with bipolar depression often becomes generational. The unhealthy and at times dangerous patterns are accepted and considered normal. As exposed children become adults, they often recreate similar patterns in their own lives and families. They seek out what is familiar, therefore, they tend to settle for relationships which are abusive and destructive, simply because this has been a part of their past.

Families with these issues cannot escape the emotional trauma without serious consequences. Prolonged stress and hurts must be coped with in some way. Each individual member of the family will develop unhealthy and defensive coping mechanisms, which often become problematic in future relationships. Avoidance of intimacy, denial of thoughts and emotions, projecting blame and displacing anger are all unhealthy defenses acquired by families with bipolar depression. Repeatedly marriages fail, families are destroyed and the core of society destabilizes from the anger, rage, and violence of Bipolar Disorder, Type II.

Leon's Story

"The purpose of these comments is to describe what it is like to live with someone who is Bipolar Type II. I have been married twice. The first lasted for 15 years. My second wife and I have been married for 19 years. I believe each of my wives suffered from Bipolar Disorder Type II.

I met my first wife, Karen, in college. While we were dating, I learned that she was very emotional. Her emotions were mainly displayed as crying fits. She would get upset easily and often. I thought that after we got married, I would be able to make her happy, and she would not have these emotional swings. Of course, that was just wishful thinking. Before we were married, her upsets were directed at other situations or persons. It wasn't long after we were married that the mood swings were directed at me. Through the years they became worse and more dramatic.

During our marriage it was almost impossible to make friends, because Karen always found something wrong with them and would often strike out at them in anger. She always had a lot of crying spells. Most of the time I would not know the cause of them, they just seemed to come on. The mood swings became so predominant, and to such a degree that I found myself walking on eggshells to try to keep them from happening. I began thinking during the good times, "when will the next upset come?"

As things became worse, she not only attacked me, she also would attack our daughter. One day I saw her kicking our two-year old across the floor. At this point I knew I had to get help. Karen's psychiatrist recommended some medication and shock treatments. At first it seemed that it helped. She would become much calmer, almost like she was in a daze. It didn't take long to realize, neither the medicine, or the shock treatments had any long-term effect.

Over the next year or so, I saw first-hand her "uncontrolled anger" towards me, at my daughter, the neighbors and store clerks. She was like a volcano ready to erupt at the least provocation. She would through dishes on the floor to break them. She would throw glasses, pots, and pans, anything she had in her hand. One evening she took her scissors and cut up all my ties. Other times she would hide my car keys, let the air out of my tires, draw on the walls with lipstick, this was anger I had never seen before. Because of her unpredictable behavior, I would call home several times a day to see how things were going. I did not want our daughter to be hurt, and if Karen sounded out of control, I would go home. One day Karen overdosed on her meds and was hospitalized for three weeks. After this, I was transferred to a new city for work.

I remember having the hope that the new environment would somehow help the situation, again wishful thinking. It was at this point that Karen began drinking. The house was a mess most of the time, as it seemed that not much mattered as long as she had her alcohol. On three occasions I got her to go to a rehab facility, but she did not complete any of them. After that my daughter and I moved out of the home. Separation then divorce didn't eliminate the problem, as I was continually getting phone calls from her needing help or threatening suicide.

Karen never did get the help she needed. She did get help with the alcohol problem but never help with the bipolar. She now lives alone in a slum area of a city. She has no friends except for a house full of cats. I understand that her house is a complete wreck and smells of cat urine to such an extent that people cannot even walk into it. I'm told that she still has rages of anger with neighbors, store clerks, and most anyone with whom she comes into contact. Karen has spent a complete lifetime of being out of control emotionally and miserable. What if Karen had been given the right therapy 50 years ago? Could there have been a saved life?

Following 15 years of single life, I married again and again to one who was bipolar. Of course, I did not know this when we got married. She had been my high school sweetheart and we had not seen or communicated with each other for over 30 years. At first, I did not see the bipolar characteristics in her.

From what I know, I would characterize both Karen and Barbara as Bipolar Type II. Barbara was never physically abusive, nor what I would call "out of control." She did have extreme emotional swings, sometime for reasons unknown to me. She would become verbally abusive, but never threw things at me or threatened me physically.

Barbara seemed to have, just beneath the surface, this anger that would very easily burst out. It would be displayed most of the time in nastiness, and "put-downs". This was mainly directed at me, although on occasion others would be in the line of fire. Sometimes, her words would be more directed at me, like "I wish you were dead," or "wish you would just go to hell."

Like with Karen, it become so that even in our good times, I would wonder when the next upset would come. Barbara realized that our marriage was a roller coaster but she actually thought that was normal. When she was growing up, her family was always that way and she told me once that she just didn't know how to have a life different than that.

One other thing, which I had no idea was happening to me was the fact that all the stress of living in this manner was killing me. In just six years before seeking therapy, I had surgery for a quadruple bi-pass, although I had absolutely no warning signs such as high cholesterol or high blood pressure. Following that, I had to have a heart stent. Then, I had to have two heart stents, then two more heart stents. I developed bleeding ulcers in the stomach resulting in extremely low blood count. Soon after that I was diagnosed with cancer of the bladder, had surgery for it, and received chemo. Cancer was eliminated. But I soon developed bladder cancer again and had surgery once again followed by chemo. Next, I was hospitalized for internal bleeding followed by dangerously low blood count. Then came surgery for a herniated disc in my back, a blood clot in my right leg, which resulted in another surgery. Then I was hospitalized for Guinan-Barre, which left my lower legs and feet numb. Next came congestive heart failure, followed by sleep apnea. I mention all of this because I believe, as does my therapist, that nearly all, if not all of this, was the result of the tremendous stress under which I was living. Because of the therapy I have received, I have learned how to handle stress, but more importantly, the stress within our family has significantly subsided.

A year ago, I would have said that our marriage, if it did continue, would always be a miserable one. Today [with Barbara getting help], we are both happy in our marriage and feel very confident about our future. Without this help, I have no doubt that our lives would have continually deteriorated until death. And the rate I was going, death was right around the comer. Today, I feel really great and my heart muscle strength has returned to almost normal for a person my age. It never could have happened if I were still living in a completely stressful situation.

People do not have to live 50 years in misery, as my first wife has done. Having lived with one who received no help for her bi-polar (resulting in over 50 years of misery) and with one who received help for her bipolar type II, I can personally testify that no one has to live a lifetime in misery as a result of bipolar disorder. Why waste one more day in misery when it is not necessary?" Leon.

CHAPTER 2
Understanding Mood Disorders

"I am writing this letter [to my father] in order to help me find some peace in my life. To find closure to all the pain, but most importantly ... so you can understand how traumatic your one decision has disrupted my whole life, altered my normalcy and for the most part, destroyed my childhood. Hopefully, you will read this whole letter, not just for me, but so you too, can also feel peace, as I am sure your lack of responsibility in your children's lives must have at some point haunted you," Tina.

Defining Normal Moods

Mood problems have been in existence since the beginning of time and they occur as frequently as the common cold. The term mood disorder refers primarily to severe and chronic sadness or a depressed emotional state. Low moods or periods of sadness are not considered to be depression, unless they interfere with ordinary life. Normal sadness will occur following any significant loss. A family death, a significant financial or job loss, severe marital or family problems are all conditions which create feelings of sadness and despair. These emotions are normal and consistent with misfortune and the many trials of life.

Most sadness resolves over a brief time period. However, sadness from close and personal losses will generally take longer to subside. Healthcare practitioners often see sadness or mild depression in connection with painful illness and injury. As medical conditions such as these improve, so does any associated sadness or depression. It is also normal to feel frustrated, angry and sad when an important goal in life cannot be reached. Even young children demonstrate sadness and anger when something they want is denied or withheld from them. These are all examples of what constitutes normal and ordinary mood changes that occur from ordinary life events.

Types of Mood Disorder

The time frame and intensity of mood changes will determine normal from abnormal conditions. Normal remission of most emotional states such as anger, sadness or mild depression will vary for each individual. Minor emotional conditions may resolve in a few moments, while sadness from the loss of a loved one could take many months to improve.

Mood disorders have two basic causes, which involve both biological and psychological factors. The biological aspects are concerned primarily with genetics and heredity. This means that certain families and their members are susceptible and mood disorders can be passed from one generation to the next. However, not all who are genetically predisposed actually acquire an illness. The psychological aspects tend to be learned. These learned behaviors, may also pass from one generation to the next and involve negative thinking patterns and behavioral modeling.

The following list of mood disorders is given below to help increase general awareness of these common conditions.

1. *Major Depression*
2. *Dysthymic Disorder*
3. *Bipolar Disorder:*
    a. Type I
    b. Type II
4. *Cyclothymiacs Disorder*
5. *Pediatric Bipolar Disorder or Temper Dysregulation Disorder.*

Major Depression is the most common mood disorder. People with major depression have a prolonged period of sadness or low mood. Generally, there is an absence of mood swings such as highs and lows. The lows can last for several weeks or longer. Sleep and appetite patterns are usually affected. People with major depression tend to eat either too much or too little. Weight loss is common and many people with depression will experience nausea from the thought of eating.

On the other hand, major depression can result in weight gain. These individuals overeat and tend to gravitate toward foods with a high-carbohydrate content. Binge eating foods such as pasta, pizza and sweets is very common. Therefore, weight gain is a symptom of major depression just as weight loss. These food related problems tend to develop into eating disorders such as anorexia, bulimia and obesity.

For the overeater with an underlying depression, food becomes a substitute for antidepressant medications. These individuals crave food that contains sugar, which generates a brief psychological high and alters the unpleasant mood. The elevation in mood is very brief, however, it provides temporary relief from sadness and despair. This is followed by a crash in mood, which usually occurs from an over consumption of sugar. This, unfortunately, leads to a deeper state of depression and increased appetite, which keeps the cycle going.

The symptoms of major depression also include loss of motivation and lack of desire to engage in the daily activities of life. The depressed person tends to isolate from others and has diminished social contacts. The severity of low mood causes days of missed employment and diminished job performance. A decrease in sexual desire is also seen in people with major depression, which adversely affects marital relationships. These people tend to cry easily and frequently. They are overly sensitive to stress in their lives and frequently cry when challenges arise. Others tend to respond by becoming emotionally numb and detached.

Dysthymic Disorder, also a very common mood problem, is described as a low-grade depression. All of the symptoms, behaviors and problems outlined above for major depression occur in dysthymic disorder. The difference being that dysthymia involves lower intensity and duration of symptoms.

Bipolar Disorder is more complex than major depression or dysthymia. The lows are present as they are in depression. However, other symptoms exist such as elevated mood, racing thoughts, irritability, anger and rage. There are two types of bipolar disorder, Type I and Type II. Type II is the most under-recognized problem in healthcare today. This book is devoted to increasing awareness of this serious and in some cases life threatening illness.

The Bipolar Disorder, Type I has been identified and successfully treated for many decades. The highs and lows of type I have been recorded in the medical literature for centuries. Type I includes periods of mania, and overreacting to events in their world. Mania has many distinct symptoms, which include rapid speech, high energy levels, racing thoughts and a decreased need for sleep. People with mania tend to go on unrestricted spending sprees, and they may engage in dangerous business endeavors. These behaviors can last a number of weeks or even months before it cycles back into depression. The symptoms of Type I are easily identified by the patient, family and healthcare professionals. Treatment is often effective and includes medications with psychotherapy. However, many people with Bipolar Disorder, Type I say they enjoy the highs and they often resist attempts at treatment, which may eliminate them. They view the highs as periods of great productivity and creativeness.

Cyclothymic disorder includes most of the Type I bipolar traits but to a much lesser degree. The moods cycle from high to low, speech becomes rapid, thoughts may race and the need for sleep will lessen. Individuals with cyclothymic disorder have greater ability to control their behaviors, since they are not as severe. The elevated mood also cycles into depression however, the cycles tend to be less severe than those seen in manic-depression.

It is important to understand that mood disorders are not associated with weakness in one's personality, nor, are they caused by dysfunctional parent-child relationships. They do have many psychological components, particularly sadness and mild forms of depression, which are derived from negative thoughts and perceptions. Anxiety, which is a clinical term for fear, also has psychological causes. Irrational and unrealistic thoughts associated with ordinary life events will generate fears and anxiety.

    The moderate-to-severe forms of mood disorders have a strong biological basis. That means certain chemicals located in the human brain play a major role in all of these disorders. For example, it has been scientifically proven that serotonin levels have a significant impact on mood. A delicate balance of serotonin levels must be maintained between brain cells in order to prevent the occurrence of depression. A chemical imbalance resulting in reduced levels of serotonin will produce a clinical depression. Most antidepressant medications used today are designed to help restore the delicate balance of serotonin levels between cells in the brain.

    The bipolar mood disorders are more complicated with several more brain chemicals involved. These mood problems also have serotonin involvement along with others, such as dopamine and norepinephrine. The imbalances of these additional brain chemicals associated with bipolar conditions produce an increased number of observable symptoms. In order to maintain normal and stable moods, a balancing act of all brain chemicals is required. This equilibrium and chemical balance is determined by the genetic makeup of the individual.

> *More recently, children have been diagnosed with bipolar disorder. Prior to this, most children with anger, temper and rage problems were considered to have a conduct disorder or attention deficit disorder. Conduct disorder of childhood included chronic behavior problems such as fighting, stealing, rebellion at home and school, and impulsiveness.*

Children with attention deficit and hyperactive disorder also have similar problems such as low frustration tolerance and impulsivity. These children get frustrated easily, abandon tasks and frequently fail to complete academic assignments. The younger children with attention deficit also display brief temper tantrums when they become frustrated.

These anger and rage problems have been associated with more severe forms of conduct disorder or attention deficit disorder by clinicians treating pediatric populations. It wasn't until the 1990's that the mood component was identified in these children and the separate diagnosis of pediatric bipolar disorder was established.

Children with severe anger and rage problems also have periods of depressed mood. They tend to cry easily and often appear sad, their moods cycle between sadness, irritability, anger, rage, and hyperactivity. Most of these children have a positive family history of mood disorders, including bipolar disorder and substance abuse. The causes are the same as adult bipolar mood disorders and they are linked with genetic and biological abnormalities affecting the central nervous systems. The new Diagnostic and Statistical Manual (DSM) will include the pediatric bipolar condition, however the terminology will change to Temper Dysregulation Disorder. The reason for change has to do with elimination of a clinical label, which tends to stigmatize the child for life.

The important message here is that children can develop mood problems. Misdiagnosing a pediatric mood disorder as a conduct disorder or attention deficit disorder results in improper treatment. The true mood problem worsens over time and the child becomes an adult with serious anger and rage issues.

Heredity determines the genetic composition of all human beings. Unfortunately, the genes responsible for mood stabilization can be flawed, placing the person at high risk for mood problems at the moment of conception. This genetic predisposition usually remains dormant until some major event takes place in the person's life. A major event creates a high level of stress, which in turn triggers the defective genes responsible for the mood disorder.

Stress is an unavoidable part of life and it has a significant impact on general health, especially in today's world. Many other health related problems such as heart disease and hypertension are directly associated with stress. Exposure to excessive stressful events can lead to an array of human illnesses including bipolar depression.

It is important to also understand how physical conditions; headaches, muscle aches and chronic pain all tend to accompany depression. Fibromyalgia has become much more common among people with depression. Usually, the depression is masked or hidden within the physical symptoms. Patients tend to focus more on the physical problems and fail to recognize the underlying depression. On the other hand, a clinical depression often becomes secondary to physical illness and injury. The underlying depression often lies dormant, until physical injury or a health condition occurs. At this point, psychological, in addition to medical intervention is necessary.

The good news is that most mood problems including bipolar depression are correctable. Healing for those with Bipolar Disorder, Type II begins with a good differential diagnosis and effective treatment strategies. A combination of medication and psychotherapy works best for all mood disorders. Medications or therapy alone often fail to achieve optimal therapeutic results. Much more needs to be said about therapies for mood disorders, therefore, a more detailed discussion of treatment approaches will be given in chapter six on "healing methods".

Tina's Story

"This year I just turned 47 years old. I am writing these comments to my father for abandoning me because of my mother's Bipolar Disorder Type II. I have two beautiful boys, both now grown. I have a successful business and a very nice home. For the most part, I guess you would say that I am a very blessed woman, and I would agree. I have only one problem and it is a big one. I am emotionally dysfunctional.

I am writing this letter [to my father] in order to help me find some peace in my life and to find closure to all the pain, but most importantly... so you can understand how traumatic your one decision was. It disrupted my whole life, altered my normalcy and for the most part, destroyed my childhood. Hopefully, you will read this whole letter, not just for me, but so you too, can also feel peace, as I am sure your lack of responsibility in your children's lives must have at some point haunted you.

The earliest memories were around 4 years old. You and Mom were in the front yard screaming at each other. Mostly, she was screaming. You were pulling her across the lawn by her hair and kicking her. I do understand why you left a hostile situation like that. It was not good for any of us. That doesn't mean you should abandon your children.

Shortly after that, I can remember laying in bed or standing at the front door crying for hours and just repeating over and over, "I want my Daddy!" You were never there. On the rare occasions that you would come, you would take us to your parent's house and leave us there. Sometimes though, you would take us to Shelia's and we would play with her kids, the children that you chose to raise instead of your own. Can you imagine how painful that was? Knowing that your Dad would rather raise and watch grow up, someone else's children? Can you feel the pain of the rejection? You can't use as an excuse that Mom made it too difficult. You made the choice to have children. It was your responsibility to take care of them. We were not disposable goods.

When we were living in the housing project, Mom had to tell us that there was no Easter Bunny or Santa Claus. She didn't want us to think we were bad children because we never got baskets or had gotten the toys we wanted at Christmas. I still wonder what Shelia's children Christmas' were like. Christmas is still a very sad time for me.

At age 5, I believe, that is when Mom attempted to commit suicide. So now, I didn't have you and mom is trying to leave us too. Did you take us? We both know the answer to that.

I lived with my aunts for a while, and I don't remember seeing you once. My brothers and I were placed in foster care. We were in a huge two-story farmhouse. From the outside you would have thought, what a great place to live. It was grand and beautiful. But, let me tell you what happened there. Our foster mother wanted to be called Aunt Bee. Well, Aunt Bee was anything but mothering. She was a very abusive woman. On one occasion, to punish me, she got out the wooden brush. The kind you would use with the old fashion dustpans. Only this one, she cut all the bristles off of it. She beat me with it from the dining room, up a spiral staircase and all the way into the bedroom. I cried all night because it hurt so badly to simply lie there. On another occasion, I was not hungry for dinner. I was not aware what the punishment was for refusing to eat, so I had to find out the hard way. Dinner that night was vegetable soup. I came to learn that if you didn't finish by the time everyone else was done, you wore your dinner. [Aunt Bee] dumped the soup straight over my head and then I had to sit there wearing it and freezing until bedtime. Before going to bed, I had to clean it all up prior to getting myself cleaned up. I had all of these wonderful memories by the age of six. I feel so robbed. Where were you?

    I will never forget the day we were told that Mom was better now and was making arrangements to get us back. I thought life was going to get better now. She had met someone who was also a patient in the facility she was in. At first I thought we were going to have a normal life like other kids. We had our Mom back and someone who wanted to be our Dad. I don't think normal quite cuts it. In some respects it was.

We had family dinners and went on vacations together. The family dinners were very nice. Before he came along, we didn't really have dinners, so to speak. It was a treat for us to have meat on the table. Most of the time, it was pasta because that was the cheapest thing that you can raise three kids on. I can remember the child support battles. You were fighting it every step of the way. Again, you were raising someone else's three kids and didn't want to contribute to the welfare of your own.

The big problem was, this new man met Mom at the [psychiatric] facility and he was there for alcohol abuse. I am not sure how long it had been before he started drinking again. That led to yet again, Mom getting beaten. This was a regular event, although he never hurt us kids, physically. He would do other things that were not particularly pleasant.

At age 8 was the first time I had the horrible experience of knowing what being molested was. Yes, I was sexually abused. I didn't tell anyone for years. I was ashamed and I felt it was all, "my" fault. Not only that, but that would mean we wouldn't be a family anymore. The biggest thing was, would Mom try to commit suicide again and this time, succeed? What would happen to us kids again? Where would we go? I had no one to turn to. I should have had you [my father]. We should have had you!" Tina.

CHAPTER 3

Bipolar Disorder, Type II: The Misdiagnosed Problem of the Century

"I spiraled into depression. I just couldn't figure out what was wrong. Why was I acting this way? Did I have no strength, no will power? Was it that I didn't have enough faith in God? Why couldn't my husband try to be encouraging instead of critical? I went on anti-depressants in my 30's. They did help some. But I still struggled. I thought about dying all the time, couldn't wait to die. I was overwhelmed with feelings of hopelessness, guilt, fear, and anxiety. I despised myself, thought my mother was right when she told me I was

useless and would never amount to anything. I went so far as to try to commit suicide twice. Obviously the antidepressants weren't helping me," Laurie.

"Living with Bipolar Disorder Type II is exhausting, fearful, emotional, and sad. Exhausting by constantly attempting to measure up, not ready or qualified for responsibilities required... fearful of not measuring up, wondering when there will be an outburst of anger, what is the atmosphere like today, up or down... disappointment, at not being able to pursue my personal goals," Lynn.

"Miraculously, which I believe was divine intervention, I was finally diagnosed with Bipolar Disorder, Type II and pretty severe generalized anxiety disorder. This illness was explained in-depth to me and I was encouraged to look beyond all the prior attempts at treatment because this condition is so commonly misdiagnosed, even by the best. I was very sick and skeptical to put my trust into anyone else, but something inside said to give it another chance. Thank God I did, because the new medicines began to work after a few months. The therapy was also beginning to work because it was focusing on my irrational thinking and *my high level of codependency I was living with all these years of my life,"* Phil.

Misconceptions of Bipolar Depression

Most people hear the phrase "Bipolar Disorder" and there is instant panic. Today the fearful reactions of patient and family to a "bipolar" diagnosis are similar to a cancer diagnosis. Many behavioral health clinicians are uncomfortable telling a patient they have a bipolar mood disorder, so they tend to avoid the subject altogether. As a result of this diagnostic phobia, poor detection and inadequate treatment protocols, patients and their families are suffering needlessly. Unfortunately, many of these cases often result in suicide. Losses of complete families from murder and suicide have become regular media headlines. It's time for society to take the blinders off and face this very treatable medical condition.

Bipolar depression is commonly confused with ADHD, anxiety disorder, explosive disorder and even major depressive illnesses. Hearing the term "bipolar" triggers thoughts such as "psycho", "crazy", "nut case" and even "insanity" when all of these labels are the furthest from the truth. It is not "manic-depressive" or "schizophrenic" or any other term implying that the afflicted person needs to be "lock-up". It is simply a very common mood problem that can be identified and corrected within a reasonable time period. Because of the social and healthcare denial of this condition, it can progress if untreated to a critical and sometimes life threatening state. When it is diagnosed and treated correctly, the symptoms are gradually reduced and often eliminated. During the initial months of therapy medications begin to work by correcting chemical imbalances and regulating cellular functions of the brain. Cognitive therapies should also be initiated to help control and alter negative thoughts associated with sadness and fear. Later, as emotional stability is achieved, intensive therapies can be utilized to heal the deeper co-dependent issues often present with bipolar depression.

Bipolar Depressions vs. Manic-Depression

As mentioned previously there are two primary bipolar conditions, Type I being the most common and most recognized in clinical practice. All of society is familiar with Type I, which is referred to manic-depressive illness. It has a genetic cause and is treated medically and psychologically. Medical therapy usually includes a medication such as Lithium to stabilize the highs and lows. Often times other medications are included as needed such as anti-depressants, anti-anxiety and anti-psychotics in the more severe cases.

A host of books, websites and other media have devoted volumes to the discussion of manic-depression. Many books have been written by, both, famous and un-famous authors, who have been exposed to this unfortunate illness. The most up to date references attribute Type I to a strong genetic and hereditary etiology or cause. Symptoms may begin in early adulthood and generally manifest following exposure to a prolonged stressful event.

The term "bipolar" has been coined to exemplify two distinct and opposite ends of the emotional spectrum. Bi, meaning two or polar, refers to an end point which seems appropriate, when describing such an emotional and volatile condition. For the person with Type I, there are few periods in life when their mood is stable. The highs and lows can be mild, moderate or severe depending on the seriousness of the illness. It is important to keep in mind such mood changes are caused by chemical imbalances in the brain, which are predetermined genetically. This explains why certain medications have been so successful in controlling the extreme volatility of moods.

Manic-depression can be a very serious and debilitating health problem. Many who have it are placed on medical and psychological disability due to a pronounced inability to function in everyday life. Manic and mania are synonymous terms. They describe an uncontrollable high, which can last for days, weeks and sometimes months. As the high reaches an eventual plateau, a deep and dreaded major depression sets in and often lasts a proportionate amount of time. This represents the emotional cycle of life for people with Type I, bipolar disorder.

Bipolar Disorder, Type II, or bipolar depression, the primary focus of this book, is an undiagnosed epidemic of anger and rage, which has permeated most of society and very few are linking it with this potentially serious mood problem. As a result, many lives are being devastated and lost due to murders, suicides and abuse of all kinds. School shootings, random violent attacks, domestic violence and self-abusive behaviors are all symptomatic of bipolar depression.

Here are the basic facts to keep in mind. Hardly a family in this country escapes some contact with Bipolar Disorder, Type II and serious harm often occurs unnecessarily to family members, as well as to the patients themselves. The problem is genetic and it is an inherited condition, although, not everyone in the family develops the illness. Imbalances in brain chemistry, not personality weakness is the root cause of the disorder, and stress is the triggering mechanism.

Basic Symptoms of Bipolar Disorder, Type II

Here are the basic symptoms to keep in mind when considering bipolar depression in the family.

1. Mood swings: Mood changes can occur very rapidly with little warning. These changes are unpredictable and erratic. Often times, trivial events can trigger a dramatic change in mood. Family members may become overly cautious and feel as though they are "walking on egg shells".
2. Hypomania: (hypo means low and hyper means high) Hypomania refers to a low-grade manic episode. Moods occasionally become elevated and the individual may become more talkative than usual, with increased energy and diminished need for sleep.
3. Depression: Depression is commonly observed in Bipolar Disorder, Type II. Sadness and

depression manifest as a decrease in energy and loss of motivation. There is a tendency to cry easily, avoid social contact and to isolate for extended periods of time. Attempts at suicide are made during this deeply depressed emotional state.

4. Racing thoughts: A very common symptom of Bipolar Disorder, Type II is racing thoughts, which refers to a steady flow of ideas. The mind is seldom at rest. It is this failure of the mind to rest, which causes the sleep disturbances of Bipolar Disorder, Type II and contributes to anxiety.

5. Irritability: Irritable mood is a common symptom of Bipolar Disorder, Type II. The patients are often described as grouchy and miserable to live with. They are unsettled and have difficulty relaxing. Irritability and a lack of cooperation with others is commonly reported in people with bipolar depression.

6. Agitation: Agitation is also common in Bipolar Disorder, Type II. Often times, agitation leads to episodes of rage and violence, especially when the patient is under stress. This symptom should be taken seriously, because most abusive and violent acts are preceded by periods of agitation.

7. Rage: Raging is a common occurrence by people with Bipolar Disorder, Type II. This is the most serious symptom, because both domestic and social violence often occurs as a result of bipolar rage. Tirade is another word, which is synonymous with rage. The tirades can become uncontrollable. Verbal and physical abuse often ensues and most violent crimes against society, family and self originate out of this rage.

Stress is a Trigger for mood disorders

Medical literature has well established the fact that stress acts as a catalyst for many health problems. Some of the more common medical conditions triggered by stress include hypertension (high blood pressure), heart attacks, increased susceptibility to viral and bacterial infections.

Prolonged periods of stress may also cause an increase in behavioral health problems as well. For example, anxiety and depression can manifest quickly when highly stressful situations are encountered. Stress can trigger alcohol and substance abuse. Most mood problems such as bipolar depression have been associated with exposure to stressful events.

Stress alone is not the sole cause of the illness. A

person must have acquired the genetic predisposition or have inherited the genes from one or both parents at conception. The genetic factors are responsible for the biological predisposition of type II bipolar disorder. Adding stress produces chemical and hormonal changes, which result in the manifestation of symptoms. Also, Bipolar Disorder, Type II can be present in one's genetic make-up and never result in actual expression of symptoms.

These individuals are typically seen as "carriers" of the illness. Another family member may inherit the genetic make-up and develop all the symptoms after a brief encounter with a stressful event. Sometimes, several decades of life may pass before the symptoms emerge. In other instances, the symptoms present themselves in childhood and adolescence. There are no specific age ranges for bipolar depression. It occurs in young children through old age.

Defining Stress

Stress is best understood as forces from the outside world affecting the individual. Often, stress is unavoidable and simply a part of life, however, stress does not always have a negative influence on health and life. Individual reactions to stress vary considerably and differ according to each person. The behavioral and physical forces of each person are interacting with the external stressors to achieve some balance. This generally results in a positive outcome where constructive change takes place.

A key to understanding the negative effects of stress requires an understanding of the concept of "internal environment". All living organisms strive to maintain a steady internal state. Biologists refer to this as homeostasis. In other words, external stress will alter the internal state, which is constantly working to reestablish balance or the steady state.

Researchers have identified powerful neurotransmitters that are released in response to stress. Neurotransmitters are the chemicals that carry messages to and from the nerve cells. This is the point at which stress begins to adversely affect mood. Due to inherent deficiencies, the body is unable to restore chemical balance because incorrect messages are sent between the cells. At this point those who are predisposed to bipolar depression begin to display symptoms. Unfortunately physical and emotional responses become extreme. Once triggered the symptoms can be very difficult to stop. Irritability, agitation, anger and rage ensue with abuse and violence as the behavioral manifestations.

Too many primary care and behavioral practitioners often miss the Bipolar Type II diagnosis, which can result in catastrophic outcomes. For some odd reason, Bipolar Disorder, Type II has failed to reach professional and public awareness. Misdiagnosis and improper treatment approaches have contributed to an epidemic of family abuse and social violence. It is now time to bring this serious problem into the forefront and help prevent further destruction of human life.

Laurie's Story

"I was diagnosed with Bipolar Disorder Type II at age 47. What a relief to find out what was wrong with me, and to know that there was help out there. All those years I wondered if I was crazy. I couldn't figure out how I could be on top of the world one minute and in the pit the next.

I was raised primarily by my mother and she was Bipolar, to the extreme. She was also an alcoholic, a mean alcoholic. She made life for us kids horrendous. We lived in terror every day. She would fly into these rages that turned very ugly very quickly. For some reason I took the brunt of these rages. I was the middle child, and supposedly her favorite. You couldn't tell by me. I was beaten every day, over and over. She beat me in the head with steel pots and pans. She kicked me, punched me, and even strangled me once. If my sister hadn't come in and stopped her once I would be dead, as I was already blacked out at that point. She would cut off chunks of my hair while beating me with the neighbor kids looking in the door watching the whole thing. She was very abusive verbally. I was never praised, even if I brought home straight A's on my report card. The chores I did were never done right. I was never encouraged or supported in any way. I couldn't wait until I was 18 so I could get out of there.

I did leave immediately when I was 18, but the damage was done. I had no self-esteem. I considered myself a big loser. None of the nice guys wanted to date me. I was pretty hyper. I talked the loudest of anybody in a group. And I talked really fast. Because my thoughts were racing, racing, racing it was difficult to carry on a conversation with me. I jumped from one thing to the next. No one could follow what I was saying. People were always put off by how I acted. I was very lonely.

A minister friend got me to go to a Christian College. The people there were a lot nicer than those in high school. But I was still on the outside looking in for the most part. I tried to fit in but most people didn't want to get to know me because of how hyper I was. Then a friend set me up on a blind date and I met this guy who seemed too good to be true. I couldn't believe a man like him could be interested in me. We got married 10 months after we first met. That's when life became hard. Now, my moods and behavior affected someone else. I became more aware of how different I was. At first I accepted help from him to change into a better person. Then I decided I liked who I was well enough and didn't want to change any more.

When our first child was born I became very afraid. I was tormented by terrible nightmares of my mother. I was petrified of turning into her, but determined that I wouldn't be like her. Now life became "very" hard. In some ways, I succeeded in my determination. I was never physically abusive. But mentally was another story. I had a very sharp, sarcastic tongue. That was damaging.

I spiraled into depression. I just couldn't figure out what was wrong. Why was I acting this way? Did I have no strength, no will power? Was it that I didn't have enough faith in God? Why couldn't my husband try to be encouraging instead of critical? I went on anti-depressants in my 30's. They did help some. But I still struggled.

I thought about dying all the time, couldn't wait to die. I was overwhelmed with feelings of hopelessness, guilt, fear, and anxiety. I despised myself, thought my mother was right when she told me I was useless and would never amount to anything. I went so far as to try to commit suicide twice. Obviously the anti-depressants weren't helping me.

Over 15 years had passed since I was put on the anti-depressants. Although some things were better, I was really worse off than ever. I was sure I was crazy. I thought those steel pot hits in the head had caused some sort of brain damage. It was time to do something else. I got in contact with a new psychotherapist we had seen earlier for some problems with our child.

Then came the diagnosis of Bipolar Disorder Type II. Then came medication, which is extremely important to take on a regular basis. Then came lots of therapy. At last, help and hope arrived. I am doing so much better. I am still in therapy working out a lot of "stuff." But life now looks promising," Laurie.

Lynn's Story

"Living with Bipolar Disorder Type II is exhausting, fearful, emotional, and sad. Exhausting by constantly attempting to measure up, not ready or qualified for responsibilities required...Fearful of not measuring up, wondering when there will be an outburst of anger, what is the atmosphere like today, up or down... Emotional days and nights either very high or very low; "walking on eggshells," with few conversations not ending in emotional extremes... Sadness or helplessness, having Mom cry on my shoulder, hearing parents quarrel, and seeing them mistreat each other... Feeling disappointment at not being able to pursue my personal goals," Lynn.

Phil's Story

"My story begins with a highly dysfunctional family. My father was an abusive alcoholic and my mother has a severe mental illness, which was thought to be schizophrenia. She was highly unstable emotionally and her thinking was usually bizarre and inappropriate. She was usually in a paranoid state of mind and was unable to be a nurturing parent. In fact, she became abusive, neglectful, and was an embarrassment. My father would drink alcohol regularly and was violent while he was drunk. I was hurt tremendously both physically and emotionally by both parents.

I grew up thinking there was something wrong with me and I never really felt comfortable socially. I was usually comparing myself with others, trying to match up and deep down feeling very insecure. I was becoming highly codependent early in life.

Despite all the abuse, neglect, divorce of my parents, and codependency, which I was unaware of until more recently, I graduated from high school and entered one of the top universities in the state. As a business and finance major, I was challenged tremendously throughout college. I first noticed my high levels of anxiety and mood changes during this time of my life. These problems remained and progressively became worse over time.

I guess it was a gift of intelligence that kept me functioning because I graduated, married, and became very successful with our family-owned business, which my wife and I started after we were married. The marriage itself became disastrous due to our highly controlling and codependent personalities. I began to have severe mood swings, periods of uncontrolled anger and rage, which ultimately played a part in our divorce.

I ended up losing the business and my home to my wife. She took primary custody of my only child. I began to spiral in deep depression, high anxiety, and a heightened sense of agitation, anger, and rage. My mind raced continuously out of control with all sorts of irrational thoughts and ideas. Ultimately I was disabled by this illness, and recently learned I was suffering from Bipolar Disorder, Type II. After years of seeking help from psychiatrists, psychologists, and counselors, I was progressively getting worse. I have to admit that I am lucky to be alive today given all the hopelessness and suicidal thinking I experienced.

Now to the most important message I hope to convey. Through years of receiving help in the forms of therapy and a spectrum of medications, nothing really worked until I was finally diagnosed with Bipolar Disorder, Type II. I was given every diagnosis imaginable because of my failure to respond to treatment. I was treated by some of the brightest and most qualified doctors who became frustrated with my failure to respond. They began to take it out on me by saying things like I was genetically defective, never would improve, and I was destined to a lifetime of chronic impairment due to mental illness. I was really treated badly in several instances, which compounded my problems. This phase of my life went on for years without any end in sight.

Miraculously, which I believe was divine intervention, I was finally diagnosed with Bipolar Disorder, Type II and pretty severe generalized anxiety disorder. This illness was explained in-depth to me and I was encouraged to look beyond all the prior attempts at treatment because this condition is so commonly misdiagnosed, even by the best. I was very sick and skeptical to put my trust into anyone else, but something inside said to give it another chance. Thank God I did, because the new medicines began to work after a few months. The therapy was also beginning to work because it was focusing on my irrational thinking and my high level of codependency I was living with all these years of my life.

I was always told I wasn't bipolar because I didn't have clear-cut manic episodes. In other words, I was told I didn't have Bipolar, Type I, but I had never even heard of a Type II diagnosis. I now understand how misdiagnosing this problem can be devastating to the patient.

Today, I am functioning better than ever. The symptoms are controlled for the most part. I am back functioning at the same type of business and I feel good about myself, and the direction my life is taking. I realize the illness is often genetic, hereditary, and highly vulnerable to stress levels, which I have learned to constantly monitor. I am taking very little medication today and I see all kinds of potential for my life personally and professionally. Without the diagnosis of Bipolar Disorder Type II, I might not have been here today to write this story," Phil.

Chapter 4
Abuse in the Family Associated with Bipolar Disorder, Type II

"When I met my ex-husband I had no idea what Bipolar Disorder Type II was. I had heard the term, but never really gave it much thought. I knew that Tom was unstable and abnormal, and I figured that I could fix him. I was so naive. His destructive behavior and irrational thinking will more than likely continue to take a toll on my life and the life of our daughter for years to come. No matter what boundaries I put up, I will never be able to escape the scars he inflicted," Terry.

Disrupted Family Systems

Healthy families are the basic building blocks of any culture or society. As families encounter excessive amounts of stress, they approach a breaking point. The effects are not only family based, but also, they adversely affect society at large. As previously discussed, some stress is inevitable and can generate productive change. The family stress associated with abuse seldom has a positive or beneficial effect. On the contrary, reaching the breaking point signals the beginning of a disrupted and dysfunctional family system.

The overall objective of this book is to help prevent families from reaching the breaking point. Those families who have gone beyond this point can clearly benefit as well by instituting change to help reverse the dysfunctional family patterns caused by rage and abuse. Recognizing the root problem as an undiagnosed type II bipolar condition is the prerequisite for change.

Not all disrupted families have bipolar depression as the central cause. Remember stress can have a similar effect on the family unit as it does on the individuals. Families are systems. Roles are assumed and assigned. Goals and objectives are established. Communication patterns are essential to maintaining a viable system. Most external and internal stressors will clearly impact the functionality of the system by influencing any one or all of these factors.

Common Sources of Family Stress

Illness of any type, whether behavioral or physical, tends to create stress on the family. Other external sources of family stress include employment changes, geographic and location changes, even recreational travel tends to be a family stressor. The emotional and physical health of the family system generally determines how well coping and adjusting to these stressors takes place.

Many common individual sources of stress frequently occur within families. Husbands and fathers, like wives and mothers, have multiple roles and responsibilities, all of which can become quite stressful. As children develop, they also acquire new and potentially stressful roles and responsibilities. Any major impediment or inherent problem such as bipolar depression can significantly alter coping mechanisms. The result may very well be the creation of a highly dysfunctional family with some form of abuse at the core.

The Family Abuser

The primary effect of Bipolar Disorder, Type II on the family is abuse. Both males and females tend to be equally susceptible; therefore, the abuse may come from any family member. Keep in mind that children are not immune. Often, a pediatric bipolar depression exists with most of the adult symptoms present, including rage and violence. The abuser may even become one of the children, who take their anger and rage out on parents and other family members.

A common phrase expressed by a family member when describing an episode of rage is "going off". This means a tirade takes place with ranting and raving over some issue. Very little, if any communication or problem solving takes place during an episode of rage. Excessive agitation and anger are clearly released, however, the anger is projected in a damaging way onto family members. The abuser finds fault, and externalizes blame while in a tirade with others.

A very interesting dynamic takes place at this point, which needs further elaboration. Most abusive people with bipolar depression are unaware of what is happening to them both physically and psychologically. They experience negative emotional responses internally and attribute them to some external event, not realizing that the intensity of the emotion is governed more by internal factors rather than the event itself. This is justification for their frequent accusation and blame, which is often placed on others. They falsely accuse and fail to recognize the true culprit, which is stress, and the inability of the body to naturally regulate chemical and hormonal imbalance. This is the hallmark of Bipolar Disorder, Type II.

Types of Family Abuse

Abuse of family members from bipolar rage is consistent with the degree of illness. In other words, the more severe forms of this condition often result in serious abuse of all types. Milder forms of abuse are present in less severe cases. Never the less, abuse is damaging and destructive to the victim regardless of degree.

Substance abuse is common with bipolar depression. Unfortunately, an attempt at self-medication with drugs and alcohol only magnifies the anger and rage. Thus, the tendency for more excessive abuse is increased with the inclusion of substances. Families are at greater risk for harm whenever alcohol and drug abuse are introduced into the picture.

Family abuse often takes several forms. Initially, uncontrolled anger and rage will generate verbally abusive patterns within the family. Isolated events may lead to more frequent and intensive episodes of abuse. Family tolerance builds, allowing the abuser greater opportunity to become more abusive. Also, the level of fear increases which contribute toward greater unhealthy tolerance of the abuse.

Verbal abuse in the family gradually evolves into physical threats. The threats may escalate into throwing and breaking objects. In the more severe cases, bipolar anger and rage, will frequently lead to physical abuse and injury to a family member. Most of the domestic violence seen today has its roots in these episodes of rage, associated with bipolar depression.

Substance Abuse and Bipolar Depression

The abuse of alcohol, drugs and food has increased to epidemic proportions throughout our nation. Children are experimenting with substances at younger ages and many become addicted before adulthood. Large segments of this childhood population have been raised in abusive or neglectful families, with at least one parent suffering from a mood disorder and substance abuse.

Children and parents, who are predisposed to mood problems such a bipolar depression, become substance abusers with little awareness of their underlying mood issue. Many of these parents have been self-medicating for years with drugs, alcohol and food. Unsuccessful attempts at recovery from substance abuse result in greater frustration, hopelessness and increased despair. This is referred to as a "cycle of abuse", where mood and substances progressively worsen over time.

Often times, an underlying anxiety and depression are identified along with substance abuse. Treating the mood disorder and the addiction simultaneously produces a more successful outcome. However, many unsuccessful attempts at recovery from addiction occur and frequently they tend to be the result of undiagnosed Bipolar Disorder, Type II.

Antidepressant and anti-anxiety medications are not effective alone with bipolar depression. Unfortunately, most cases are treated in this manner because clinicians today are unaware of the diagnosis. This lack of awareness should not be confused with incompetence or malpractice. There simply has not been enough media attention from professional or public sources. If your family member has the symptoms of Bipolar Disorder, Type II along with some form of substance abuse, make sure the mood disorder is correctly identified and treated. This will contribute significantly to a more successful recovery from most types of substance abuse and addictions.

Abuse and the Family Scapegoat

Abusive relationships in the family generate highly dysfunctional patterns, which are often characterized by poor communication, frustrated need for love, and lack of acceptance. Abuse damages confidence and creates self-destructive behaviors in the victim. The rage and violence of untreated bipolar depression creates dysfunctional patterns, and also sets the stage for development of a family scapegoat.

The scapegoat, or the "black sheep" in the family, is identified to bear the brunt of family conflict and turmoil. The abusive member through his or her anger and rage generates frustration and fear in others, which is displaced primarily onto one person in the family. The member of the family identified as the scapegoat is often seen as problematic. Typically, they are brought into therapy as "the designated patient" and the family focuses on this person with all their complaints.

The abusive parent or sibling, oddly enough, is seldom viewed as problematic and they are rarely confronted. They are too volatile, easily angered, and prone to rages. Therefore, others "walk on egg shells" around the abusive family member. Thus, the family avoids more abuse by choosing someone, who can tolerate their displacement of fear and anger. Direct confrontation of someone with bipolar depression seldom produces beneficial results. A scapegoat is needed by the family for projection of their own dysfunction.

It is not uncommon for the strongest, healthiest and most capable family member to become identified as the scapegoat. The abuse creates a high level of stress on the family and they need an outlet to survive. Many of the negative thoughts and feelings of the family get projected onto the scapegoat. This is an unconscious process, which develops over time, as the abuse persists.

The family scapegoat becomes open to sarcasm, ridicule and criticism by the family. The degree of negative attention usually parallels the intensity of abuse by the bipolar member. This is not done as intentionally as it may appear. An abused family will develop unhealthy patterns, many of which they are unaware. Creating the family scapegoat is one of those patterns.

A common belief of a family scapegoat is, "I can never fit in." The family creates an atmosphere of rejection for this person and fitting in socially also becomes an issue over time. Guilt, anxiety and depression may become lifelong issues for the family scapegoat, until they receive effective behavioral intervention.

Finally, a child who has bipolar depression and has one or both parents with the same disorder can also become the family scapegoat. In this case, the inflicted parent and child develop serious relationship problems and the child becomes the problem of the family. This family has greater stress and dysfunctional patterns, which are projected onto the child. Given this child's greater stress level, identification as scapegoat and inherited mood disorder, they enter into a life-long history of substance abuse, vocational instability, serious relationship problems, and in some cases, death from suicide.

Terry's Story

"When I met my ex-husband I had no idea what Bipolar Disorder Type II was. I had heard the term, but never really gave it much thought. I knew that Tom was unstable and abnormal, and I figured that I could fix him. I was so naive. His destructive behavior and irrational thinking will more than likely continue to take a toll on my life and the life of our daughter for years to come. No matter what boundaries I put up, I will never be able to escape the scars he inflicted.

The problem is not solely that he is Bipolar. The challenge is, he remains undiagnosed and refuses to seek any help at all. He is very comfortable in his lonely place called "denial". Tom has a lot of the classic signs and symptoms you associate with Bipolar, such as fits of rage, irrational thought, compulsive behavior, racing thoughts, a false sense of euphoria and invincibility, along with bouts of low depression. Tom is a master manipulator and an expert con man. He was able to talk his way out of any sticky situation and I always fell for his lines.

Throughout our relationship the biggest source of trouble was his compulsion to gamble. At first it started out as a fun recreational activity then, it quickly escalated and spiraled out of control. When he would run out of funds he would beg me for money. If I didn't have it he would steal my things and pawn them. I remember coming home one day and finding my expensive game console missing. When I confronted him about it he apologized and said he pawned it so he could pay his portion of the rent. When he saw I was still angry he tried to use seduction as a tool to manipulate. A couple days later I came home and my TV, VCR, and DVD's were all missing. I remember becoming so angry, yet I never had the good sense to leave. I later found out he was using the money he made at the pawnshop to gamble. When the items of value were all gone he forced me to write bad checks by threatening harm or saying he would leave me. Looking back I realize I would have been better off if he had left. Unfortunately, at that time I was in too deep to see the reality of the situation.

    After awhile his compulsion to gamble subsided a bit. Mostly because I had moved out, but I believe a part of it was the fact he had come down from his manic episode. He started sleeping more, drinking heavily, and crying a lot. I thought he was feeling remorse. Maybe he was, I will never really know. After seeing the change in his behavior, I decided against my better judgment, to give him a second chance. He was desperate to have me back in his life so he threw me every line he could. I fell for it and we were married. I was also pregnant. For a very brief time, maybe a span of 3 weeks after the wedding, life was grand. He was kind, considerate and excited about our child. He even got a job. That all changed in the blink of an eye. He started staying out with friends till 2, 3, or even 4:00 in the morning. The first few times I thought nothing of it, then, I grew tired and confronted him. He would become so angry towards me, telling me how I was trying to control him and ruin his life. He would throw things, all the while screaming every derogatory name he could muster from his limited vocabulary. After a particular instance where he became more physically violent toward me, I decided it would be safer if I kept the peace. Peace at any cost became my mantra. As a result I became physically ill, I was put on bed rest to safeguard my pregnancy. I lost my job and along with it my only sense of security, It was a dark time for me and I remember thinking I'd never see a light on the other side of the tunnel.

A few months after I lost my job he was sentenced to a prison term for an armed robbery. I felt so relieved. I knew we would be safe now. Unfortunately, the judge gave Tom 30 days to tie up loose ends and put his affairs in order. At that time I had about three thousand dollars saved up to live off of while I was out of work with the baby, Three days before Tom was due to go to prison he disappeared and took my debit card with him. By the time I realized what had happened all the money was gone. I was devastated. At 34 weeks pregnant I lost 9 pounds in 3 days. Betrayal, pain, anger and resentment had become close friends of mine. I shut down. At 4 am, five hours before he was due at the courthouse, Tom came home.

Although these are distant memories, the pain is much too fresh. Even after the divorce he continues to try and destroy my peace and wellbeing. I continue to work through the pain and I am determined to get to the other side. I continue to face the monster, each time my head is held a little higher with the knowledge that I am the only one who can control my inner peace," Terry.

Chapter 5
Bipolar Disorder, Type II and the Development of Codependency

"The rages came often and so would the fits, holes punched in walls, he would hurt my feelings, and I realized he had turned into his father. When I confronted him on his behavior, he would say in the calmest voice that there's nothing wrong with him. It was me that had the problem. For many years I had to tiptoe around him, not incite him to go off in a fit of rage. He was like a giant toddler trapped inside a man's body," Patty.

"I've spent the past few years going through many periods of depression without really knowing what was causing it. I lived with anxiety that at times made me feel like I wanted to just scream and take off running. There were actually times when I would do both. I would run until I could not run anymore. A few months ago, I hit the lowest of lows, it was by far the deepest depression I had ever been in. I just wanted to crawl in a hole and die. I don't know why, but for some reason I knew that I needed help, I needed to conquer this beast once and for all. I was withdrawing from friends, family, and my wife," Eric.

Codependency History

The term codependency has been associated with addictions and substance abuse for decades. There is a vast network of co-dependency support groups nationally and around the world, which focuses on helping families cope with the long term effects of alcohol and drug abuse. They also help direct attention to the personality traits of a spouse or family member, who contributes to the addict's destructive behavioral patterns through a process called "enabling". It is the enabling pattern in the family which becomes synonymous with co-dependency.

Co-dependency is a highly important subject matter for families who have been exposed to anger, rage, and the abusive behaviors stemming from bipolar depression. The focus of co-dependency has always been in connection with the drug and alcohol abuse and seldom in association with underlying mood disorders. These mood disorders are usually responsible for self medicating behaviors such as drug and alcohol abuse. Therefore, it is essential to generate awareness of co-dependency through books, research, magazine articles, seminars, as well as increasing the network of support groups available to the public.

Co-dependency problems are as common as cold and flu viruses, which permeate all of society. This chapter is an attempt at bridging the gap between bipolar depression and co-dependency. The reader needs to be aware of the highly codependent behaviors that evolve in all families touched by anger, rage, abuse, and neglect of undiagnosed bipolar depression.

Personality Traits of Co-dependency

Below is a list of symptoms along with some helpful examples of personality traits associated with co-dependency.

- People pleasing: If there is one common denominator in co-dependency, it is the overwhelming attempts at pleasing others. The people pleaser typically overextends him or herself to ensure others are satisfied and in agreement with their actions. They are highly sensitive to facial expressions, verbal comments and the actions of others.

- Walking on eggshells: Most co-dependent people become extremely cautious around significant others. The phrase "walking on eggshells" was created to describe the reluctance one has to create any frustration or anger in those with whom they are most closely associated. Tip-toeing around others, attempting to keep the peace by saying and doing what others expect of them reflects the deep seated fear of anger and rage.

- Difficulties confronting others: Most co-dependent people have strong fears of confronting others and they avoid situations which require assertiveness. Confrontation carries a very negative connotation, rather than an actual constructive purpose, which is to assertively present one's important thoughts and feelings to others. Confrontation is often viewed as engaging an enemy, resulting in verbal and in some instances physical encounters. Thoughts, feelings and personal needs are all too often repressed out of fear of retaliation or harm. The inability to appropriately confront others causes sadness, frustration, and depression in the co-dependent person.

Negative Thinking

A very common trait of co-dependency is negative thinking. Thoughts which are unrealistic, illogical, irrational, and at times lies, are considered negativistic. The causes of negative thinking are linked directly with emotional and physical trauma. Exposure to hurts and trauma shapes ones thoughts around the unpleasant event. Gradually, negative thinking becomes the norm regardless of the situation.

The negative thoughts of co-dependency can be projected onto people and situations without direct awareness. Highly co-dependent people generally fail to realize the extent of their negative thinking. They are very accustomed to finding faults and seeing the worst in most situations.

Fears and Anxiety

Anxiety and fear are synonymous and interchangeable terms describing a highly unpleasant emotional state. Anxiety is a clinical term used when fear has been present for prolonged periods of time. Anxiety can be focused specifically on one object or one situation. It can also be generalized. In other words general fear and anxiety seem to occur in most situations, and they are unpredictable.

Fear and anxiety are at the core of co-dependency, which governs how a person responds to the environment. The most common behavioral manifestation of fear is avoidance. Fear generates avoidance of conflict at any expense. It has been explained in previous sections how prolonged exposure to verbal and physical abuse creates fear of asserting oneself, and avoidance of difficult situations. Fear is also at the root of what has been referred to as people-pleasing and peace-keeping traits.

The co-dependent person becomes hyper vigilant to their surroundings. This means they are externally focused and have fear of focusing on themselves. Their external focus is learned and becomes a self protective mechanism aimed at preventing explosive and abusive behaviors by others. A common perception of the codependent person is "If others are ok, then I will be ok." There is little awareness and capability of caring for oneself emotionally. The essence of co-dependency is the fear of rejection and loss of external love.

Love and Co-dependency

The human need for love is present from birth and exists throughout the life cycle. Parental love helps to meet this need from early childhood and facilitates healthy emotional development. Lack of adequate love is experienced as rejection, which takes many forms including neglect and abuse. Physical, emotional, and sexual abuse all damage and inhibit emotional development. Failure to adequately satisfy the childhood need for love will eventually evolve into the development of co-dependent personality traits.

An unmet need for love during childhood creates lifelong attempts at satisfying this need through many external sources. In other words, the co-dependent adult strives for love, acceptance, and approval, just as the young child depends on parents and caretakers for the same love. Human beings have only one opportunity during childhood to meet this basic need for love. If unmet, a very high level of co-dependency on others becomes central to every significant relationship in their life.

The experience of love during childhood is critical to the development of confidence, security, and ability for self-love. Many hear the term self-love and equate it with selfishness and narcissism, when in fact it represents acceptance and self-approval. The lack of love apparent in co-dependency creates overly critical thinking, disapproval, and rejection of oneself, all leading to impaired emotional development. Thoughts become irrational and unrealistic, which leads to fear, sadness, and despair.

The most common irrational belief is "If I can please the significant others in my life, they will, in turn, provide me with the love I so desperately need." This is a false perception of how intimate relationships are designed to work. Little attention is given to oneself as the co-dependent person focuses primarily on pleasing others for love. The analogy of having a low "love tank" has been used by many to describe the essence of co-dependency.

The inability to fill this "love tank" independently forces the co-dependent individual into unhealthy relationships consisting of abuse and neglect. The life of a co-dependent person evolves into an unequal balancing act of trying to meet the needs of others for approval and acceptance while ignoring their personal and emotional needs. This becomes a chronic and lifelong condition, which progressively worsens over time resulting in the development of anxiety and depression. Most people with co-dependency require psychotherapy and a period of treatment with anti-depressant medication to heal from this painful and debilitating condition. Primary psychotherapy goals are to reduce dependency on others, and to improve the ability to love oneself.

Patty's Story

"When I met my husband 30 years ago, we both worked in his father's restaurant along with a few of his siblings. They told me his father was manic-depressive and to be aware of his mood swings. We had to walk on eggshells around him to keep him happy. It wasn't obvious to me at first as he kept himself in-check. He seemed to me a charming, respectful hard-working man. It wasn't until years later when I saw for myself how he could change from a charming person to a violent abusive person. I learned he was someone to watch out for and stay away from during his simmering rages. It didn't take much for him to rage on, sometimes throwing things that were in his way.

I noticed change in my husband when his father died. He started to take on his father's mannerisms. I recall saying to his sister how he was "turning into his father." She said, "in what way?" and in denial, I couldn't explain nor elaborate. He would leave to go to work in a great mood and two hours later when I showed up for my shift, he would be this angry man on a rampage. When I asked him what happened he would be upset over a pot of sauce that was left out.

The rages came often and so would the fits, holes punched in walls, he would hurt my feelings, and I realized he had turned into his father. When I confronted him on his behavior, he would say in the calmest voice that there's nothing wrong with him. It was me that had the problem. For many years I had to tiptoe around him, not incite him to go off in a fit of rage. He was like a giant toddler trapped inside a man's body.

I didn't realize that Bipolar Disorder, Type II was a disease, and that this disease could pass from generation to generation. Now, I have to hope our children don't end up with their father's sickness," Patty.

Eric's Story

"My name is Eric, I've spent the past few years going through many periods of depression without really knowing what was causing it. I lived with anxiety that at times made me feel like I wanted to just scream and take off running. There were actually times when I would do both. I would run until I could not run anymore. A few months ago, I hit the lowest of lows, it was by far the deepest depression I had ever been in. I just wanted to crawl in a hole and die. I don't know why, but for some reason I knew that I needed help, I needed to conquer this beast once and for all. I was withdrawing from friends, family, and my wife.

My depression started when I met my wife, about 8 years ago. It was a very stressful time, with us dating, and her dating other people while still seeing me. I could not understand it, but I just put my head down and ran, full throttle towards the goal which was being with her. I fell in love hard, and she fell in love with me. We made our life together and moved away from where we both called home to settle in another state. I had given up family and lifelong friends to be with the one I loved. At first it was a beautiful thing, being together, loving each other. Then something happened, my anxiety that had been so great turned to depression. I didn't know it at the time but this would be the turning point for me, and our relationship. I started taking meds to try and cope with the anxiety, and they helped, but I felt dull and not myself.

About 6 months before we were to be married my wife asked me to stop taking the meds. I agreed, consulted my Dr. and came off the antidepressants. The withdrawal symptoms were horrible, night sweats, mood swings, brain shivers, they were all very real. We had some difficulties around the wedding, but I told myself that everything would be better after we were married. The night before we were married, a close friend asked me "Eric, are you truly happy." I told him, "don't ever ask me that question again, as long as she is happy, I'm happy." That should have been a sign to me but as you know the signs aren't as obvious to the person locked into the situation. Little did I know we were living in a codependent relationship and she most likely has a mild to moderate form of bipolar depression.

We spent the first year together and had quite a few problems. We both were second- guessing our relationship and marriage. We worked on it together and chalked it up that the first year of marriage is difficult. So we started marriage counseling and I got back on some meds. This helped and soon we both were feeling better. Our lives were moving forward, traveling, working, just living and enjoying life. In the back of my mind I knew that I didn't want to be on a medication to make me "feel better". So I talked to my wife and told her I wanted to come off the meds. She said she was very apprehensive of me doing that because things were better and I was easier to deal with when on medication. I did it anyway because I did not feel like myself. So the process started again.

A year or so after coming off the medication the second time, I started to have some anxiety. We had quite a few life changing issues, cancer scares, losing jobs, difficult economy, etc., I fell into depression again. This brings us back full circle to where I realized I needed help. I called a friend and he recommended I see a professional as soon as possible.

I started therapy and was eager to learn and correct this problem. I knew I could not keep living like I had. I worked on myself for a couple of months, trying to balance the delicate marriage that was crumbling before my eyes. One night my wife came to me and said we needed to go to marriage counseling. I said great and we went. The marriage counselor basically said to her that she needed one on one therapy for herself so she could see the role she was playing in our marriage. She said that "your husband is already going and the longer you wait the farther behind you are going to be." The marriage counselor said to her that we were living in an unhealthy codependent relationship and that if she doesn't take some responsibility for what was going on, we are most likely going to end up in a divorce. She did not want any part of it. My wife said she did not have any problems to work on, that we had problems, because they were mine. I begged her to go to therapy, worked around all her excuses, in the end she blamed my mother saying she caused all the problems in our marriage, and blamed me for treating her like crap. All these behaviors I have learned are common in a relationship with someone with Bipolar Disorder Type II.

I never could understand how if someone loved you, why they would always blame you for everything. I remember having conversations with her, she would say something that genuinely hurt my feelings, and I would confront her. She would turn it around on me and tell me that it was my fault that she was treating me the way she did. I would sit there and for the life of me could not understand why it was my fault for feeling hurt.

I've been in therapy for over a year now, and it still hurts me today to say that our marriage did not last.

We have been divorced for almost nine months. She came to me and said that we have too many problems and she doesn't see it getting any better or ever changing. She chose a different path. It is still extremely difficult. I realize now I was living with someone that was abusive. She had an abusive personality and it is very damaging to one's self worth and overall wellbeing. I work on myself daily, and find I still to this day have second thoughts about all that I did. I maybe could have tried harder to convince her that she needed help. In the end, I know these aren't realistic thoughts, but the codependent side of me is still trying to make everything right, the protector, and the fixer.

I've also realized that this is a pattern with someone like her. A friend called me about two months after we were divorced and told me he had seen her with another man about two weeks after the divorce. It took me a while to get a grip on this. I still have a hard time to this day. I remember asking her when we were going through the divorce if there was someone else, she looked at the ground and said no.

I've since put everything together and realized that's why she did not want to get help, she had already started to move on with someone else before we were even divorced. This is a control issue, when she had lost control of me, she needed to move to the next person, and something she could have control over. It still hurts me to think how much I loved her and yet she could do the things she did and make me feel guilty for her actions even when I knew I was not responsible. I still felt guilty.

I'm here to say today that things get better, I'm not going to sugarcoat it and tell you that it is a great ride and all, it is the hardest most difficult thing I have ever done. If my story sounds familiar, the best advice I can give you is to seek professional help and love yourself. Know that it does get better and you will heal from this. It is not easy but you will love the person that comes out the other side," Eric.

Chapter 6
Process of Healing from Bipolar Disorder, Type II

"Imagine spending 35 years of your life in the dark. That's what it felt like to me from the age of 15 when I took my first overdose of pills. I took my second overdose at the age of 21 and ended up in the state psychiatric hospital. It was then that I was first treated for chronic depression. Over the years I've been on many medications for depression; Lithium, Prozac, Effexor, Zoloft and others that I don't remember. And even while taking these medications, something was always wrong as I suffered from severe mood swings where I would be fine one minute and angry at the world the next," Ellen.

"I am a person diagnosed with Bipolar Disorder, Type II. I remember being stunned initially by the diagnosis and didn't fully understand it. Eventually, I realized for the first time in my life that my behaviors and emotions where due to this problem. At this point, I began my journey in recovery. I made a decision to take control of my life, deal with my issues, beat my mood problem and codependency, and learn to live a productive life," Jim.

"Therapy has been a humbling and grateful experience for me that has helped to shape me into the healthy person I am today. I needed to get to that place back then where I had to admit, yes, I am suffering from Bipolar Disorder, Type II. And even that took months to get to. But, I came to realize that the diagnosis did not define my core. I am thankful my body chemically normalized within a couple of months, which allowed me to go deeper into therapy," Mary.

Dynamics of Hurt and Emotional Pain

It has become evident that families of patients with bipolar depression develop highly dysfunctional coping patterns. The family member with untreated hurt and emotional pain develops unhealthy behaviors, which contribute to the family discord. It stands to reason that families cannot function properly when one or all of the members have been exposed to excessive emotional and physical trauma.

All family members will contribute and participate in unhealthy dynamics. Seldom does any family member escape these negative experiences. The adverse effects, upon the individual, results in ongoing relationship problems, academic difficulties, substance abuse, and employment problems. Intimate relationships within the family suffer due to lack of trust. Low confidence and poor self-esteem contribute to learning problems and general lack of academic achievements. Employment history often includes absenteeism, loss of wages, and low productivity.

Prior to healing and recovery the family must recognize the dysfunctional nature of its own existence. Most families fail to identify the degree of pathology and they tend to accept unhealthy patterns as normal family functioning. The initial phase of healing requires some level of recognition that the unhealthy patterns exist within the family. Without treatment individual family members unconsciously seek out similar dysfunctional patterns, which are integrated into relationships outside of the family context. Ultimately, they recreate the hurts and emotional pains of the original family. This becomes generational until altered through some form of therapy. It is not unusual to observe three to four existing generations all with highly codependent family members.

Codependency is at the core of these dysfunctional family patterns. Treating the codependent aspects of each personality within the family is necessary for most healing to occur. Also, keep in mind that the genetic causes of bipolar depression creates a generational problem within the family. The abnormal genetics, which predisposes individuals to a mood disorder, becomes the generational issue. Therefore, the anger, rage, and abuse remain part of each new family. These bio-psychosocial factors are cyclical, deeply rooted and highly destructive to affected families.

Unfortunately the majority of families affected by Bipolar Disorder, Type II fail to receive needed health care to recover from the abuse and codependency. Lack of social and professional awareness of bipolar depression is at the root of this problem. For those who become conscious of their own need for treatment and make a concerted effort to obtain it, healing will take place in two distinct phases.

Initially, recognizing that a problem does in fact exist often leads to consultation with a primary care health provider. Some people may bypass the primary care clinician and proceed directly to a behavior healthcare specialist with certain identifiable complaints. At this point, it is imperative that the practitioner identifies the anger, rage, and abusive behaviors through a detailed medical and social history. The existence of a potential bipolar depression in the family can be established at this point in treatment. This generally initiates the process of healing for the family member and hopefully for the person with the bipolar illness.

To a codependent family, treating a patient with bipolar depression is immediately viewed as the solution to the problem. This thinking reflects classic codependent expectations such as "If I can fix the other person in my life, I will be ok." The individual with bipolar depression seldom views him or herself as the problem and projects responsibility for the rage and abuse onto others. Eventually, family members begin to believe they are the cause of the problems. Each member of the family must learn to take responsibility for their own issues and recognize that changing others will not correct their core codependent personality traits. It is essential to keep in mind that codependent thinking occurs, in part, due to this projection of blame.

A high level of commitment to change is required of a family member exposed to abuse. This is due in part to the depth and the intensity of unhealthy personality traits stemming from the trauma of abuse. The length of therapy is usually contingent upon the degree of abuse. The more severe forms of abuse create a greater degree of emotional harm, which requires a longer period of treatment. Never the less, the most effective process of healing takes place through individual psychotherapy. This can take six months and in some cases it can take up to two years for recovery.

Cognitive-Behavioral Therapy

Cognitive behavioral therapy (CBT) and insight therapy have proven results with family members, including the individual with bipolar depression. Cognitive behavioral therapy instituted early in the healing process helps to generate and restore emotional health. The focus of cognitive therapy is on identification and remediation of negative thoughts, which are acquired through extended periods of abuse.

The ABC's of emotion are used in therapy to help explain a behavioral science theory indicating that human emotions are generated by thoughts and perceptions of momentary situations. As depicted in the diagram, (A) represents a situation that might be encountered at any moment in time. (B) represent thoughts or perceptions of the situation. (C) depicts the emotion generated by a particular thought or perception. (D) is an added factor, which represents a response or behavior generated by an emotion. This is a step-by-step mechanism which takes place very rapidly and it is similar to a chemical reaction, whereby (A) situation_ *produces* (B) thoughts and perception → *produces* (C) emotion → *produces* (D) response or behavior.

Each and every situation we encounter will generate a specific thought. A positive thought or perception produces a healthy emotion such as joy, peace, or love. The healthy emotion generated by a positive thought produces a response, which is adaptive and appropriate in the situation. This completed mechanism as described represents healthy human emotional functioning.

The opposite also holds true for unhealthy emotional states. In this case, a situation produces a negative thought or perception, which then generates an unhealthy emotion such as anger, fear, or sadness. The unhealthy emotion produces a maladaptive or inappropriate response in the situation. This mechanism defines unhealthy human emotional functioning.

The most significant of the four factors is (B), or thoughts and perception, which takes place in all momentary situations we encounter. Positive thoughts are essential for emotional health. They are defined as truthful, logical, realistic and rational perception of situations. Healthy emotions can be generated regardless of difficulty in the situation, when our thoughts are rational, logical, and realistic. Negative thoughts are considered to be the source of distress and despair. They represent irrational, unrealistic and illogical perceptions of a situation. Unhealthy emotional states are produced by the negative thought process, which originates from exposure to rage and abuse associated with Bipolar Disorder, Type II.

Cognitive Behavioral Therapy was developed to help patients identify their faulty perceptions and negative cognitions, which are responsible for their emotional distress. Once the negative thoughts and perceptions are identified, attempts are made to reconstruct more positive thinking in order to promote a healthy emotional state. Negative thoughts can become deeply ingrained as a result of exposure to abusive behaviors. Most people are unaware of their thought process and they tend to be much more conscious of how they feel in any specific situation. It is common to observe a person trying to alter a situation in an attempt to improve how they feel emotionally. Ironically, there tends to be little awareness of the fact that it is their thinking which actually is responsible for changing the emotion.

Insight Psychotherapy

Insight Psychotherapy (IT) can be integrated with cognitive behavioral therapy to help gain awareness of the root causes connected with negative cognitions. Insight therapy guides the patient through the physical and emotional trauma, while helping to identify unhealthy thought process stemming from an abusive relationship. The focus of insight oriented therapy and most other therapeutic approaches is on the identification and correction of existing codependent personality traits. It is also used with the bipolar patient to improve coping mechanisms and to restore emotional health.

Insight therapy is based on psychodynamic theory, which is concerned with the effects of significant relationships on the development of personality. Healthy interpersonal relationships are considered essential and they have a positive impact on the maturational process. Personalities, which are governed more by rational thinking and healthy emotions such as love, joy, and inner peace promote greater personality growth. Psychological symptoms such as excessive fear, anxiety, and sadness are focused on during the process of insight therapy. They are associated with a history of abuse and trauma following a prolonged relationship with an abuser. Insight therapy helps to bring the nature of these symptoms into awareness, while giving the patient continued hope and instruction for personal change and healing.

The primary treatment goal of insight therapy for codependency is learning to love oneself with less external dependency on others for approval and acceptance. Insight therapy increases self-awareness and teaches healthy patterns of thinking, feeling, and behaving, especially towards oneself. Selfishness is often confused initially with learning to love oneself. The codependent individual has a highly deprived need for love, and tries relentlessly to please others in return for their love. It is virtually impossible for another adult to provide this love sufficiently to overcome a deep and frustrated codependent need for love.

The person undergoing insight psychotherapy becomes increasingly conscious of their need for self-love, which is differentiated from selfishness. They come to understand selfishness more realistically as a genuine lack of concern for thoughts, feelings, and needs of others. Understanding basic concepts of love such as acceptance, kindness, patience, and sacrifice are paramount to this new self-discovery. Providing love to others is more natural and understandable to the codependent person. Insight psychotherapy helps the individual to recognize and apply self-love.

Treating the Whole Family

Most families develop highly dysfunctional coping patterns when a member has undiagnosed Bipolar Disorder, Type II. Treatment for the whole family is often indicated to identify and correct these dysfunctional patterns. It is highly unlikely that any member of the family truly escapes the adverse psychological effects of long-term abuse. Therefore, a trained family therapist will bring the whole family unit into the office to begin the treatment and healing process.

Family therapists are trained in systems theory, which focuses primarily on interactional patterns of the family. Small and large groups function based on these established communicational patterns. Each member contributes to the family system and plays a unique role in how well the system functions. The emotional health of any one person can easily be influenced by the interactional patterns of the total system. Likewise, the communicational patterns of the family unit can be directly influenced by the health of its members. Needless to say, the presence of emotional volatility associated with bipolar depression creates highly dysfunctional patterns in the family. The family therapist helps to identify these unhealthy patterns and works with the family unit to restore functionality to the system.

Alternative Assistance

Most local communities have a vast network of support groups to assist with medical and behavioral health care issues. There are support groups also dealing specifically with codependency, bipolar disorder, and depression. Many of the addiction recovery groups including Alcoholics Anonymous (AA), Narcotics Anonymous (NA), and Overeaters Anonymous (OA), all provide free twelve-step recovery programs in most communities.

It his highly recommended that family members with any type of dependency or addiction stemming from bipolar depression seek alternative support assistance. Most underlying mood disorders such as depression and Bipolar Disorder, Type II is associated with substance abuse and addiction. It is also well documented that individuals with moderate to high levels of codependency also self-medicate through alcohol, drugs, and food. Fortunately, alternative assistance programs are easily assessable with little to no costs.

Medications for Depression and Anxiety

The healing process for families with a bipolar member may require medication therapies in addition to psychotherapy. Family members with moderate to severe anxiety, depression, and codependency will clearly benefit from medication therapy. Prolonged periods of stress, anxiety, and depression produce chemical in-balances in the brain. These in-balances fail to change or spontaneously resolve with psychotherapy alone. A combination treatment approach, including both medication and psychotherapy produces the best long-term outcomes for families with Bipolar Disorder, Type II.

The intent of this chapter is not to provide detailed psychopharmacology, but to provide medication guidelines for treatment. The patient with Bipolar

Disorder, Type II typically requires a mood stabilizer, an antidepressant, and oftentimes, a medication used at night to help induce sleep. The family member who requires treatment for depression and anxiety benefits from newer antidepressant medications such as Selective Serotonin Reuptake Inhibitors (SSRI's) or Serotonin Norepinephrine Reuptake Inhibitors (SNRI's). For the healthcare providers who prescribe these medications, caution should be taken when treating Bipolar Disorder, Type II with SNRI's, since they can induce an elevated mood in some patients.

In summary, a combination of medication and psychotherapy, are most effective for managing the symptoms of Bipolar Disorder, Type II.

Psychological- Various psychological therapies are useful for the treatment of this mood disorder. These include, but are not limited to;

(A) Cognitive Behavioral Therapy

(B) Insight-Oriented Therapy

(C) Family Therapy

(D) Chemical Dependency Treatment, including the 12 Step Recovery Programs.

Medications- Three classes of medication are currently available to effectively treat Bipolar Disorder, Type II.

(A) Mood Stabilizers

(B) Antidepressants

(C) Atypical antipsychotics

These are all potentially effective treatment options and should be discussed with a healthcare provider.

Ellen's Story

"Imagine spending 35 years of your life in the dark. That's what it felt like to me from the age of 15 when I took my first overdose of pills. I took my second overdose at the age of 21 and ended up in the state psychiatric hospital. It was then that I was first treated for chronic depression. Over the years I've been on many medications for depression; Lithium, Prozac, Effexor, Zoloft and others that I don't remember. And even while taking these medications, something was always wrong as I suffered from severe mood swings where I would be fine one minute and angry at the world the next.

I remember taking a weekend trip to New York City with coworkers and not talking to anyone for two out of the three days we were gone. I completely withdrew without any apparent reason. I went back to work and quit my job. I was so embarrassed and confused by my own behavior. Individual therapy sessions and group therapy yielded the same diagnosis, chronic depression. None of the therapy seemed to make any difference, just more of the same up and down cycles. These cycles impacted every aspect of my life. Relationships were impossible and it was difficult keeping a job. I ended up lonely and miserable. I was angry with myself for not being able to "get my act together."

Today, I am so much better. I was diagnosed with Bipolar Disorder Type II. For over a year now, I have been doing well. With the right combination of medications and individual therapy, I have been able to maintain a pretty normal life. I've had the same job for almost a year and a half, I'm taking online classes to get my degree and I feel hopeful for the first time in 35 years. I urge anyone who's being treated for depression and the treatment doesn't seem to be working, to look into Bipolar Disorder Type II. If I had been diagnosed correctly years ago, my life could have been so different," Ellen.

Jim's Story

"I am a person diagnosed with Bipolar Disorder, Type II. I remember being stunned initially by the diagnosis and didn't fully understand it. Eventually, I realized for the first time in my life that my behaviors and emotions where due to this problem. At this point, I began my journey in recovery. I made a decision to take control of my life, deal with my issues, beat my mood problem and codependency, and learn to live a productive life.

I have been subjected to physical, sexual, and mental abuse throughout different points in my life. If you want to heal, you need to take these life experiences and learn from them. Take the negatives and turn them into positives and move forward because you can only control your own thoughts and actions. You cannot let the actions of others dictate how you live your life.

It all started in my early childhood. The beatings from misbehaving ranged from punches to a belt and even a 2x4 occasionally. I had two incidents of sexual abuse both of which are too painful to fully remember, although both had a major effect on my life. The mental abuse ranged from "you're no good" to "you will never amount to anything." There weren't a lot of positives growing up. I was suffering from low self-esteem and acted out occasionally. In high school I was bullied a number of times and began to withdraw. I also began to be rebellious and defiant. I started weightlifting as a way to stop the bullying and it worked. I have never been picked on since that time.

My young adulthood was productive, healthy, and somewhat happy. I had a career in law enforcement. Unfortunately, I married a woman with severe anger and rage problems and was subjected to more mental abuse. My wife had Bipolar Type II and major codependency issues. She would not seek help because she thought she was 'ok' and I was the sick one. I finally broke free of this abusive marriage and am now free of her abuse.

I am sharing my story in hopes that someone might relate to these experiences and realize that whatever your situation, it is not hopeless. With the right help, you too, can understand and rise above to live with hope. I took control of my life and so can you," Jim.

Mary's Story

"Therapy has been a humbling and grateful experience for me that has helped to shape me into the healthy person I am today. I needed to get to that place back then where I had to admit, yes, I am suffering from Bipolar Disorder Type II. And even that took months to get to. But, I came to realize that the diagnosis did not define my core. I am thankful my body chemically normalized within a couple of months, which allowed me to go deeper into therapy.

I had a lot of stuffed fears and erratic behaviors that had led to Bipolar Type II. Therapy has helped me unravel dysfunctional patterns from childhood I had adopted to protect myself from the hurt and pain. During these last two years, I have learned to love myself in a wholesome and mature way. I have acquired skills and tools to help me in my everyday life. My thinking today is clear and forthright not fragmented and disjointed. I am learning how to really trust again and it feels so good and so free.

I understand now that what was not given to me by my parents back in childhood cannot today be given to me by them. It is now up to me, and God to love myself back to the wholeness I so desired. I can say confidently that I am not only a survivor of Bipolar

Disorder Type II and codependency. I have overcome the negative aspects of these illnesses as well. I believe that if I can do it, anyone who desires wholeness and health and puts in the effort can also achieve it," Mary.

Chapter 7
Social and legal consequences of Bipolar Disorder, Type II

"Part of Paul's legal case has included showing a history of Linda's mental illness. This history includes; recent and past alcohol/drug abuse and stays in detox, recent outpatient treatment for chronic and severe bulimia nervosa, years of severe mood disorders, addictive behaviors, inpatient mental health treatment programs, medications, and therapy. Linda also was transported to the hospital for losing consciousness while taking care of their five-month-old daughter. Linda's problems also included criminal charges including, discharging a firearm in the home, domestic violence, and shoplifting," Paul.

The Criminal Justice System

Untreated Bipolar depression has created a tremendous burden on the criminal justice system. Ironically, the system currently has little awareness of this mood disorder. The vast number of cases appearing before the courts continues to steadily rise due to repeat offenders and new undiagnosed cases entering the system. Many cases are directly associated with crime involving drugs, alcohol, and violent acts against society.

There is little awareness of the mood problem, which underlies most repeat drug and alcohol offenses. Many of these alcohol and drug-related crimes including driving under the influence and motor vehicle deaths are committed by people with moderate to severe forms of mood disorders .The judicial system must become increasingly aware of the fact that self- medication with all types of substances occurs on a regular basis by those appearing before the courts for these offenses. Most courts engage in meaningful effort to curb such crimes through fines, social programs and incarceration. These are all logical consequences and highly appropriate for the committed offense. However, long-term outcome could improve significantly if underlying mood problems were addressed.

The Anger Management Approach

Most domestic violence offenders are required to participate in a regional anger management program following their arrest. These issues have been discussed in other chapters and need continued elaboration, as many families become serious victims of this growing social problem. Family members must be conscious of the fact that anger and rage problems are generally associated with bipolar depression. These uncontrolled emotions will not resolve from therapy or group counseling approaches because biological underpinnings are fueling the emotion. Anger management teaches excellent coping techniques for the average person. Unfortunately, it is not the average person who is a domestic violence offender. Individuals sent by the court to anger management programs typically have a mood disorder with a biological basis. A more focused approach correcting the mood problem needs to be taken by the anger management programs, in addition to teaching coping and stress management skills.

Individual family members of a domestic violence offender need to be on continuous alert for future episodes of rage and violence. They need to be aware of this heightened risk, despite attempts by the courts to correct and eliminate the potential for repeat offenses. Paying fines and attending anger management seminars must be combined with appropriate medical therapy for a bipolar depression. Treatment with a mood stabilizing medication is essential. Otherwise, the family remains at risk for potentially life threatening abuse.

Drug and Alcohol Counseling Approaches

The criminal justice system has become a frontline in the battle against substance abuse and violent crimes. For decades, community mental health programs have worked in conjunction with the criminal justice system to deal with these offenses. Programs, which treat substance abuse as part of criminal rehabilitation, provide sound principals and approaches to these complex behavioral problems. Lacking in this rehabilitative process is a more comprehensive understanding of the role played by undiagnosed bipolar depression.

Families need more education concerning the importance of treating underlying mood conditions, especially for a family member referred to drug and alcohol treatment. Failure to correctly diagnose and treat the mood disorder will result in a poor outcome for those receiving drug and alcohol counseling. The family must keep in mind that substance abuse is generally a form of self-medication for all types of mood disorders. Receiving a correct diagnoses and appropriate medication, in addition to effective therapy reduces the need for self-medication. Therefore, the abuse of substances such as drugs, alcohol, and food will become less frequent as well as easier to manage. A decrease in criminal activities is also likely to occur, creating a safer social environment and less public money spent on prosecuting violent crimes through the courts.

Mass Murder Epidemic

Each day the media reports on some form of violent crime against society. Many of these crimes are directed at family members, co-workers, or fellow students who become innocent victims of violent rage attacks. Each time such an event takes place the same unanswered questions are raised by the authorities. There appears to be an endless search for answers with hope of identifying a cause and cure for this growing epidemic. A closer examination of the personalities of these individuals typically reveals emotional volatility, depression, verbal and physical abuse. Threatening remarks, which frequently contain violent content is often overlooked by family and associates. Agitation and irritability are hallmarks, which rapidly escalate into rage with exposure to minimal levels of stress. It is this uncontrollable rage, which manifests as mass murder and suicide.

There are many individuals who internalize the traits and symptoms discussed above, giving little warning of potential danger to others. This is not uncommon in bipolar depression. Externally, there may be an appearance of stability, while internally a raging war may exist. These individuals are likely to explode at some point with externalization of extreme violence. Their unspoken vicious fantasies may become a reality, resulting in a catastrophic event so commonly seen today in the media.

It is an objective of this family guide for Bipolar Depression, Type II to end with an explanation of the epidemic of mass murder and suicide. Dramatic media exposure and coverage of this issue is necessary, giving specific attention to the true underlying cause of the violent crime. Most families should be adequately informed after reading this guide. The media can assist through in-depth investigation of the concepts covered in these chapters. More accurate reporting to the public of the facts needs to take place.

Continuing medical education programs and other educational units for professional licensure in each state should incorporate training on bipolar depression. The criminal justice system also needs more extensive training in the identification and appropriate referral for this common mood disorder. Business and educational leaders need training to improve their understanding of bipolar depression, in order to create needed policies aimed at prevention. The escalating violence and rage epidemic should not remain unchecked. The next step in eliminating this epidemic is to bring all the facts into public and professional awareness.

Paul's Story

"Many patients suffering from Bipolar Disorder, Type II have frequent interactions within our judicial system. One patient, Paul, realized that many of his legal battles with his wife, Linda, were rooted in his wife's undiagnosed disorder. According to Paul, Linda exhibited a history of symptoms including; abuse, mood swings with rage, addictions, impaired relationships and criminal behavior.

Paul has been engaged in a two-year legal battle to gain custody of his daughter. The following are some highlights of his legal battle. He is sharing this information so that others may recognize these signs, possibly get help for a loved one, and protect the children who are often caught in the middle of legal struggles.

Part of Paul's legal case has included showing a history of Linda's mental illness. This history includes; recent and past alcohol/drug abuse and stays in detox, recent outpatient treatment for chronic and severe bulimia nervosa, years of severe mood disorders, addictive behaviors, inpatient mental health treatment programs, medications, and therapy. Linda also was transported to the hospital for losing consciousness while taking care of their five-month-old daughter. Linda's problems also included criminal charges including, discharging a firearm in the home, domestic violence, and shoplifting.

Looking back Paul should have noted some disconcerting signals. According to Paul, Linda was very manipulative and controlling. Part of that manipulation involved getting Paul to agree to a quick engagement and marriage after only four months of dating, against his better judgment. She convinced him to purchase an engagement ring that was thousands of dollars over what he could afford. Linda deceived him regarding her inability to get pregnant, and was in fact taking medication without his knowledge so that she could get pregnant.

After the birth of their daughter, Linda started having frequent episodes of binge drinking and drunkenness. Numerous times Paul was forced to remove his daughter from the home to avoid her drinking, rages and violence. In addition, there were numerous incidents of infidelity, all leading Paul to file for divorce and a parenting arrangement. During this legal battle Linda disappeared for days with Paul's daughter, finally turning up at a women's shelter, claiming she was a victim of abuse. Linda refused to return home with Paul's daughter, choosing instead to stay with friends or other males. She even attempted to move into a homeless shelter with Paul's daughter. During this time Linda has harassed Paul via phone and text messaging, calling Paul's place of employment, including the district management office. All the while, refusing to arbitrate a mediation agreement regarding their daughter.

Because of this history, Paul has been forced to incur huge legal expenses to seek custody of his daughter. He believes Linda's undiagnosed disorder and mental issues, erratic and unstable behaviors all place his daughter in a high-risk environment. However, the legal arena has only served as a forum for Linda to display highly dramatic and manipulative behaviors. Some of these behaviors include a pattern of lying and shifting personal blame to others. During this process Paul's occasional alcohol use is being used against him, his parent's have been accused of using drugs, Linda has accused Paul of domestic violence, including filing false complaints. A follow-up DCF investigation resulted in negative findings.

Paul is hoping that by sharing his story others will recognize some of the signs of Bipolar Disorder, Type II ahead of time, especially before people decide to get married and bring children into this chaotic environment. Getting a loved one help, and getting a correct diagnosis could go a long way in stemming many of the legal cases that are backlogged in our court systems around the country," Paul.

ABC's of Emotion

POSITIVE FEELINGS

A - Situation

⬇ Produces

B - Thinking/Perceptions

POSITIVE ⬇ Produces { rational, realistic, logical, truthful

C - Emotion/Feelings

HEALTHY ⬇ Produces { love, joy, peace

D - Response/Behavior

<u>ADAPTIVE</u>: Response which works well in the situation

ABC's of Emotion

NEGATIVE FEELINGS

A - Situation

↓ Produces

B - Thinking/Perceptions

NEGATIVE ↓ Produces { irrational, unrealistic, illogical, lies

C - Emotion/Feelings

UNHEALTHY ↓ Produces { anger, fear, sadness

D - Response/Behavior

<u>MALADAPTIVE</u>: Response which does not work well in the situation

Woulas Bipolar Disorder, Type II Evaluation Scale [WBPIIS]

Frequency Code: 0 = Never, 1 = Occasionally, 2 = Often, 3 = Very often

Name:

Date of Birth:

Date of Evaluation:

Instructions: Evaluate each item below on a scale from 0 to 3 based on previous and current observations.

1. Has a family history of depression   0   1   2   3

2. Has a family history of bipolar disorder   0   1   2   3

3. Known history of alcohol and/or drug abuse   0   1   2   3

4. Has a history of domestic violence   0   1   2   3

5. Family history of anger, rage, and abuse   0   1   2   3

6. Experiences mood swings to the extremes	0	1	2	3
7. Complains of difficulty sleeping	0	1	2	3
8. Problems with attention and concentration	0	1	2	3
9. "Goes off" easily and loses temper	0	1	2	3
10. People close by tend to be walking on eggshells	0	1	2	3
11. Prior arrests for domestic violence	0	1	2	3
12. Blames others for existing problems	0	1	2	3
13. Tends to be manipulative	0	1	2	3
14. Has some criminal history other than domestic violence	0	1	2	3
15. Appears irritable and/or agitated	0	1	2	3
16. Has difficulty maintaining steady employment	0	1	2	3
17. Is argumentative	0	1	2	3

18. Talks excessively	0	1	2	3
19. Irrational and unrealistic thoughts	0	1	2	3
20. Initiates fights either verbal or physical	0	1	2	3
21. The mind seems to be in a racing mode	0	1	2	3
22. Punches walls, throws objects, or breaks things	0	1	2	3
23. Has difficulty with close relations	0	1	2	3
24. Tries to control others	0	1	2	3
25. Appears sad, unhappy, or depressed	0	1	2	3

The statements included in this evaluation are primary indicators of Bipolar Disorder, Type II. Any positive response (by checking 1-3) should require further evaluation. If you have any of these indicators, please visit our website at, Helpishere.net.

About The Author
MICHAEL J. WOULAS, Ph.D.

Michael J. Woulas, Ph.D., is a licensed psychotherapist with specialties including the treatment of adult and pediatric mood disorders, attention deficit and hyperactive disorders, chronic pain syndrome and addictions. Throughout a thirty-year career providing behavioral healthcare services he has been diagnosing and treating most forms of depression and related mood disorders. In addition to his psychological education and training he received osteopathic medical training, which has augmented his skills as a clinician. He has been in private practice in southwest Florida since 1985, providing psychotherapy services to children, adolescents and adults.